BLM Forest Lands Report – 2006 Status and Condition

By:

Tim Bottomley
Forester
USDI Bureau of Land Management
National Science and Technology Center
Denver, Colorado

Jim Menlove
Ecologist
USDA Forest Service
Interior West Forest Inventory and Analysis Unit
Odgen, Utah

Suggested Citations

Bottomley, T. and J. Menlove. 2006. BLM Forest Lands Report – 2006: Status and Condition. Bureau of Land Management, Denver, Colorado. BLM/ST/ST-07/001+5000. 111 pages.

Bureau of Land Management. 2006. BLM Forest Lands Report – 2006: Status and Condition. Bureau of Land Management, Denver, Colorado. BLM/ST/ST-07/001+5000. 111 pages.

Acknowledgements

The authors would like to thank the following BLM employees for their time and support in the development of this report: Rick Tholen (Washington Office) and Sherm Karl (National Science and Technology Center).

The following individuals from the Forest Inventory and Analysis program were instrumental in providing input and review, along with technical assistance and advice, which greatly improved the quality of this report: John Shaw, Sharon Woudenberg, Renee O'Brien, Tracey Frescino, Larry DeBlander, Mike Thompson (Interior West FIA), and Mark Hansen (North Central FIA). Their efforts are greatly appreciated.

Representatives from the BLM's National Assessment, Inventory, and Monitoring Team also played an integral part in the development of this report, both in funding and other support. These individuals were: Dan Muller, Kit Muller, and Steve Tryon.

The authors extend a special thank you to Kathy Rohling (Writer/Editor) and Jennifer Kapus (Visual Information Specialist) of the BLM's National Science and Technology Center Branch of Publishing Services for doing an outstanding job in editing, layout, design, and production of the final document.

The final "thank you" is reserved for Bill Williams, now retired from the BLM, who was a primary force in the initial stages of preparation of this document. His expertise was invaluable in establishing the focus of this report.

Table of Contents

Chapter 1—Introduction

Background

The Bureau of Land Management (BLM), an agency within the U.S. Department of the Interior (DOI), administers over 261 million surface acres of public land in the western United States, including Alaska. Approximately 69 million acres, or 26 percent, are classified as forested.

The BLM manages these forested lands according to the principles of multiple-use and sustained-yield as required by the Federal Land Policy and Management Act (FLPMA) of 1976 and the Oregon and California Railroad Act, which covers forest lands in western Oregon. National priorities for these forests include maintaining and restoring forest health, salvaging dead and dying timber, providing high-quality wildlife and fish habitat, and providing economic opportunities in rural communities by making timber and other forest products, including biomass, available from vegetation management treatments.

In the spring of 2006, the BLM contracted with the U.S. Department of Agriculture's Forest Service (FS) Forest Inventory and Analysis Program (FIA) to prepare a report specific to forest lands under the administration of the BLM. The last nationwide inventory of BLM forest lands occurred in 2001 and only addressed acres of forest land in the predominant forest types. The BLM requested additional data for this report, specifically to make general statements concerning the overall condition of these forest lands.

FIA conducts forest resource inventories over the entire United States on a sampling grid that covers lands under all ownerships and management objectives, including DOI lands; FS lands; State and local government lands; and private, tribal, and military lands where entry permission is granted, and produces numerous reports annually from the data collected. FIA data provides the most consistent, accurate, and comprehensive information available on BLM forest lands.

The BLM requested a report describing the extent and general conditions, with statistical reliability measures, of the forested lands under their jurisdiction. This report does not separate BLM forest lands by resource management objective or legal status (e.g., congressionally designated wilderness areas). While some of the terminology used in the report reflects the early history of the FIA program focusing on wood supply (e.g., timberlands), no suitability or availability of BLM forest lands for commercial wood products are implied.

The intent of the report is strategic—to give the reader a broad perspective about the condition of BLM forest lands. This report should not be used as the sole source to advocate any

particular vegetation treatment or change of condition. Decisions on vegetation management objectives are made at the local level through the BLM's land use planning processes (e.g., resource management plans - RMPs).

This report can be used during the preparation of RMPs to help guide what issues should be addressed in a plan. To illustrate, an issue on BLM lands in many areas is what has been termed "encroachment" of coniferous trees into what are considered historical grass and shrub lands. For a number of reasons, such as lack of fire, domestic livestock grazing, or cyclic wet periods, there has been an evident trend of trees establishing and growing in areas that, based on earlier historical photography, were grass or shrub lands. Whether this trend is just the re-establishment of trees after an earlier disturbance or afforestation is still in debate. This report provides information that may be helpful in understanding the extent of these changes on BLM lands. However, final resolution concerning whether the establishment of trees represents encroachment or afforestation is best determined at the site or watershed level. Also, the report does not advocate any type of management for these lands. Again, decisions regarding vegetation management objectives are best established during land use planning and should be based on a multitude of resource values, including reducing fuel hazards and improving wildlife habitat.

The body of this report is divided into three chapters:

- *Chapter 1* is organized to first acquaint the reader with FIA inventory techniques and the extent of FIA plot data on BLM lands. Readers unfamiliar with forest inventory terminology are encouraged to review the Glossary section of the report. Terms defined in the Glossary will be in bold text upon first use.

- *Chapter 2* summarizes the data by major specific forest types. Each of these forest types was analyzed in the following order: extent (total acres of occurrence and general location), trees per acre, **stand size**, **stand age**, **volume** and **biomass**, **basal area**, **stand density index (SDI)**, and number of **snags (standing dead trees)**.

- *Chapter 3* takes a different look at the data by reconsolidating it by the individual States that have BLM lands. In the State discussions, the order is as follows: acres by forest type, sampling intensity, volume, and growth. Sampling errors are provided for forest land acres and volume estimates.

The results of that analysis total nearly 80 tables of data, which are provided in Appendix A. Figures from those tables are included in this report to assist the reader in quick comprehension of the material.

For the reader who wishes to view the raw data figures, the following naming and numbering convention was used in this report. The numbering of a "Figure" in the report corresponds to its specific reference "Data Table" in Appendix A. For example, "Figure PJ 1" has a corresponding data table to support that figure titled "Data Table PJ 1."

Tables that were specifically developed for this report and don't have a reference Data Table in Appendix A are labeled with the prefix "Table" (not "Data Table") and numbered according to the chapter where the table appears. The reader will find apparent mathematical errors where discussed portions do not add up correctly to the sums. These are the result of rounding errors.

The Forest Inventory and Analysis Program

Three different FIA units have inventory and reporting responsibility for States where forest land under BLM jurisdiction has been sampled by the FIA program. They are the Intermountain West FIA (IW-FIA) unit in Ogden, Utah, the Pacific Northwest FIA (PNW-FIA) unit in Portland, Oregon, and the North Central FIA (NC-FIA) unit in St. Paul, Minnesota.

Historically, FIA has collected inventory data on a State-by-State basis, completing regionally based Statewide inventories covering the entire sampling grid for a given State every 7 to 20 or more years. These historical inventories were known as periodic inventories. Beginning in the mid-1990s, the FIA program began making a transition from periodic to annual inventories (Gillespie 1999). The annual inventory samples an evenly distributed 10 to 20 percent of the sample grid in each State every year, so that every State's grid is completed every 5 to 10 years. The annual system is better able to detect changes and trends, and efforts are continuing to establish nationally consistent standards for data collection, compilation, and reporting.

As the annual inventory methods were adopted, States were gradually added to the annual system, often while the most recent periodic surveys were being completed in other States. The result is that at any given time, land managers with forest lands in many States (such as the BLM) will have data where plot intensities and time spans change from one State to another. In addition, although most of the available data are consistent between FIA units, some variables and summaries of interest may not be available in all States, or may not be completely consistent between States. These different methodologies have direct impacts on this report, but predominately on a State basis, and are discussed in more detail in Chapter 3.

Because procedures and definitions have changed over time, previously reported summaries—including those produced by FIA or based on FIA data—may not be directly comparable with the results presented here.

FIA Inventory Methods

FIA uses a two-phase sampling procedure for all inventories. Phase one of the inventory consists of a grid of sample points systematically located across the landscape. Remotely-sensed imagery (aerial photography and/or satellite data) is used to assign attributes to the points. For periodic inventories, ownership and forest cover status are assigned to phase one points; for annual inventories, only forest cover attributes are assigned. Phase two is conducted by field crews on a subset of phase one points. The plots are stratified based on the information from phase one, and weights are calculated based on the proportion of phase one points and phase two plots in each stratum.

Phase two is conducted using a mapped-plot design that was adopted by FIA nationwide by 1995 (USDA 2005a). All of the inventory data for this report use a mapped-plot design. The design consists of a predetermined subplot layout using boundary delineations, if necessary, to define different conditions. Conditions are delineated based on changes in the forest/nonforest status, forest type, stand-size class, stand origin, and stand density. The condition proportion is the fraction of the plot area sampled on each condition, and the sum of all condition proportions for a plot equals 1.0. The number and relative size of conditions on a plot determine the area represented by each condition.

Table 1-1 shows the number of FIA plots, plots with at least one forest condition, the number of forest conditions, and the total forest condition proportions for each State, along with the FIA unit that collects data for that State, and the first year of annual data or nominal year of periodic data (periodic surveys were completed over several years, so the nominal year is that in which the inventory was completed). The number of forest conditions is always equal to or more than the number of plots with forest conditions because plots may have more than one forest condition. The total forest condition proportions is always less than or equal to the number of plots with forest conditions because some plots may have forest and nonforest conditions. Since the majority of plots have one condition, these three numbers are usually similar. The total number of plots includes plots that have forest land, nonforest land, water, and plots not accessed because of hazards or denial of access by owners or managers.

Table 1-1. FIA plots and forest conditions on BLM land.

State	Total plots	Plots with forest conditions	Forest conditions	Forest condition proportions	FIA unit	First annual or last periodic
Arizona	1,192	161	163	152.7	IW-FIA	A-2001
California	998	104	113	94.8	PNW-FIA	A-2001
Colorado	578	338	360	316.5	IW-FIA	A-2002
Idaho	412	36	38	33.1	IW-FIA	A-2004
Montana	398	75	81	64.3	IW-FIA	A-2003
Nevada	1,639	293	303	271.9	IW-FIA	A-2004
New Mexico	2,085	173	177	171.4	IW-FIA	P-2000
North Dakota	*	3	3	1.4	NC-FIA	A-2001
Oregon	899	267	295	238.6	PNW-FIA	A-2001
South Dakota	*	3	3	3.0	NC-FIA	A-2001
Utah	2,311	833	852	786.9	IW-FIA	A-2000
Washington	9	5	5	4.5	PNW-FIA	A-2001
Wyoming	2,879	230	245	200.5	IW-FIA	P-2002

* NC-FIA does not assign ownership data to nonforest conditions; therefore, the total number of plots (and the amount of non-forest land) on BLM land is unknown.

The sample was designed to meet national standards for precision in State and regional estimates of forest attributes. Standard errors, which denote the precision of estimates, are usually higher for smaller data subsets. Representative standard errors and discussions of plot density will be presented in later sections of this report.

There are some constraints on the reporting of forest land data at a national level. The first is that FIA is a strategic-level inventory, meaning that it is useful for large areas, and may not be representative where results are based on only a few plots. The States with the fewest plots on BLM forest land are North Dakota, South Dakota, and Washington. Consequently, inventory summaries for these States have a high sampling error. The FIA inventory in Alaska presents a different challenge. FIA data has only been collected in coastal Alaska, while the BLM manages large areas of forest

land in the Alaskan interior. Because FIA has established so few plots on BLM land in Alaska and because Alaska is so bio-geographically different than the other Western States (making a combination with other States unreasonable), the bulk of this report will focus on BLM forest land in the contiguous States in the western United States, of which there are nearly 33 million acres. Assessments of BLM forest lands in the Alaskan interior have been conducted through remote sensing rather than FIA plot measurements and are discussed in Appendix B.

Defining Forest Land

Forest land is defined as being at least 10 percent stocked (or formerly stocked) with live trees, and at least 1 acre in size and 120 feet wide (Helms 1998a). "Stocking" is a forestry expression of the extent to which growing space is effectively utilized by live trees. Different FIA units have historically used

different field procedures to approximate 10 percent stocking.

The IW FIA uses a 5 percent tree crown cover, as measured by field crews, to determine forested lands. Crown cover is the percent of total ground area "... covered by the crowns of trees or woody vegetation as delimited by the vertical projection of crown perimeters..." (Helms 1998b).

It has recently been recognized that, in practice, the lower limit of live-tree stocking may not be consistent between units, and some reported forest stands may not actually meet the minimum stocking definition. Differences between definitions of what species constitute forest, and how to define the lower live-tree stocking limits of forests, are an important reason why results from various inventories may not match. As a consequence, future compilations may result in a lower forest land acreage.

Chapter 2—Major BLM Forest Types

Overview of Forests on BLM Land

FIA has identified forests on BLM land in 14 States: Alaska, plus the 13 listed in Table 1-1. BLM manages over 261 million acres in those States (BLM 2006*), and about 26 percent, or 69 million acres, is forest land. About 19 percent, or 33 million acres of the 176 million acres managed by the BLM outside of Alaska, is forested. Map 2-1a shows where the major areas of BLM forest land in the contiguous States are located in relation to all BLM lands, and Map 2-1b shows their location in relation to other forest land in the Western United States. As mentioned previously, the bulk of this report will focus on the nearly 33 million acres of forest land managed by the BLM in the contiguous United States. BLM forest land in Alaska is addressed in Appendix B.

Forest resources are often described using a forest type classification. "Forest type" is a classification of forest land based on and named for the tree species presently forming a plurality of live-tree stocking. Forest type may also reflect an associated set of species, such as spruce/fir or pinyon/juniper. Forest types are determined according to the algorithm standardized under the FIA national program (Arner et al. 2001).

Forest types are often grouped by the growth form of the dominant trees. Stands comprised of tall-stature trees, typically usable in commercial wood products, are generally called timber types by FIA. Examples include Douglas-fir, ponderosa pine, and aspens. However, as discussed in the Background section of Chapter 1, FIA terminology was used for this report and no inference to commercial availability of these forests is implied.

Low-stature trees often have a multiple-stem growth form, and include pinyon pines, junipers, and many western oaks. Stands dominated by low-stature trees are generally called woodland by FIA. Therefore, forest types in this report are referred to as "forests" and "woodlands," and trees as "tall-stature" and "low-stature," respectively.

The typical growth form of a tree species also determines the location of FIA's tree diameter measurement. Diameter is taken at breast height (**DBH**) for forest (tall-stature) species and at the root collar (**DRC**) for woodland (low-stature) species (e.g., all juniper species except Western juniper, all pinyons, Rocky Mountain maple and bigtooth maple, curlleaf mountain-mahogany, all mesquite species, and western "scrub oak" species, including Gambel oak). See FIA field manuals (USDA 2005a) for a comprehensive list of species and the location of diameter measurement.

The term "nonstocked" is also listed as a forest type in FIA databases. These are stands that have a calculated stocking of less than 10 percent, but otherwise meet the definition of forest land. Field crews assign a forest type based on regeneration, adjacent stands, or non-sampled trees in the general plot area. These stands are also assigned a stand size of "nonstocked," leading to a common misconception that these lands constitute reforestation back-log. In this report (because it is helpful to know the likely forest type of these "nonstocked" stands), the forest type determined by the field crew was used and the stand size is "sparse stands."

---

* The BLM has a very active Land Tenure program where land ownership transfers regularly occur (either into or out of BLM jurisdiction) through purchase, exchange, donation, sale, and conveyance to States or other entities. The most current published acreages were used in this report. However, these acreages are certain to change in the future.

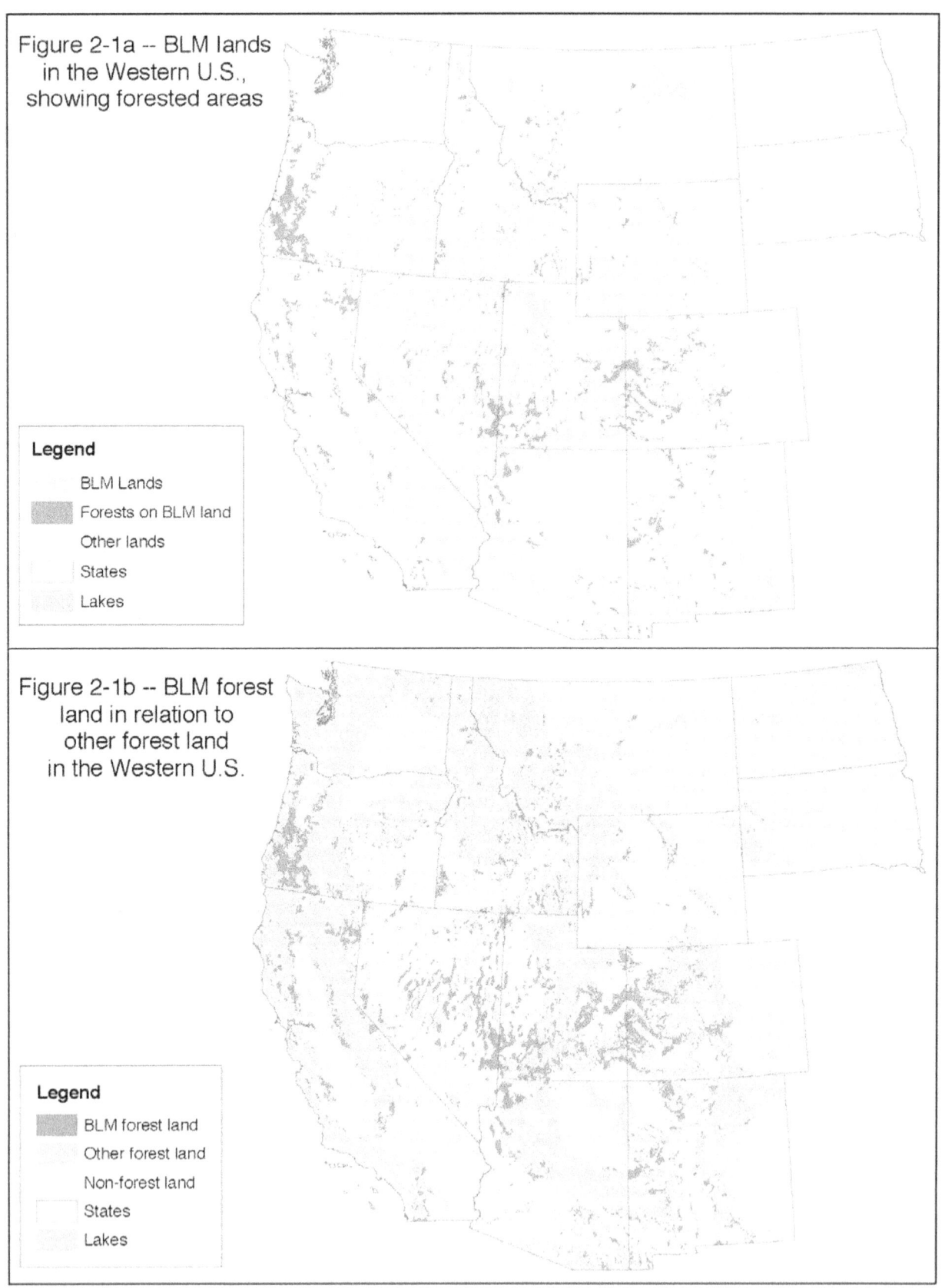

Figure 2-1a -- BLM lands in the Western U.S., showing forested areas

Legend

	BLM Lands
	Forests on BLM land
	Other lands
	States
	Lakes

Figure 2-1b -- BLM forest land in relation to other forest land in the Western U.S.

Legend

	BLM forest land
	Other forest land
	Non-forest land
	States
	Lakes

Forest Types on BLM Land within the Contiguous United States

A total of 48 different forest types were reported on BLM forest land in the contiguous United States. Appendix C provides an acreage breakdown of these forest types by State. The 10 most common types discussed in the following section account for 93 percent of the forest land acres across all States and the majority of forest land in each of the States. Table 2-1 shows the estimated acres by State of the 10 most common forest types managed by BLM in the contiguous United States. The BLM requested that FIA data analysis focus on forest conditions related to forest health, specifically stand ages and densities. These conditions are discussed for each of the 10 forest types.

As mentioned earlier, a major purpose of this report is to provide the BLM with some general information about the condition of these forest lands. While determinations of how healthy a specific forest stand is are driven by local management objectives, the information in this report can provide a general overall context of health of the BLM forest lands. Tree numbers, size, age, and density are four very broad aspects of forest health and are examined in this report.

The data include the geographic extent and estimated acreage of each of the forest types, a discussion on the number of trees per acre for an average stand in the forest type, and the estimated acreage of the forest type in each of the size classes. Each forest type is also broken out by stand-age class. Total estimated volumes in cubic feet and tons of biomass are provided for each forest type by diameter class. Data on measurements of density for each of these forest types were also needed, so each forest type is broken out by basal area and percentage maximum stand density index. Finally, the number of snags for each forest type is also provided by the size of the snags. The snag data should not be used as an indication of forest health from the standpoint of recent mortality, as these snags may have been present for many years. A better use of the snag data is a general measure of wildlife habitat.

Table 2-1. Area estimates (acres) for the 10 most common and all other forest types on BLM land in the contiguous United States. Bold entries indicate the most common forest type for a State (Note: MT includes ND and SD; OR includes WA).

Forest Type	AZ	CA	CO	ID	MT	NV	NM	ND	OR	SD	UT	WA	WY	Total***
Pinyon / juniper woodland	**1,015,050**	**303,224**	**2,852,113**	28,972	0	**5,644,277**	**946,274**	0	0	0	**5,227,447**	0	17,171	16,034,527
Juniper woodland*	520,219	136,615	652,783	139,655	35,411	1,625,783	91,968	0	0	0	1,897,674	0	**619,112**	5,719,219
Douglas-fir (all)	0	16,927	243,528	267,004	435,984		0	0	1,493,634	0	81,980	48,690	65,268	2,653,015
** *Coastal Douglas-fir*	0	16,927	0	0	0	0	0	0	**1,479,830**	0	0	0	0	1,496,756
** *Non-coastal Douglas-fir*	0	0	243,528	**267,004**	435,984	0	0	0	13,804	0	81,980	48,690	65,268	1,156,259
Western Juniper	0	277,895	0	216,921	0	55,074	0	0	1,397,669	0	0	0	0	1,947,558
Ponderosa pine	12,772	0	158,769	0	**454,194**	0	61,952	0	226,386	11,661	50,994	0	95,406	1,072,133
Deciduous oak woodland	9,579	7,904	557,958	0	0	74,848	14,802	0	0	0	299,673	0	0	964,765
Cercocarpus woodland	0	67,279	20,272	51,757	37,476	264,972	0	0	29,908	0	145,509	0	24,827	642,001
Rocky Mountain juniper woodland*	0	0	184,881	41,560	153,822	0	0	1,924	0	0	51,100	0	0	433,288
Aspen	0	0	186,794	36,718	0	30,658	0	0	25,664	0	10,919	0	77,085	367,837
Lodgepole pine	0	0	93,819	0	109,565	0	0	0	70,712	0	0	0	85,210	359,306
All other forest types	335,819	639,352	125,523	162,722	63,538	135,607	5,543	8,445	544,707	13,733	59,995	30,136	306,083	2,431,203
Totals***	1,893,439	1,449,197	5,076,439	945,309	1,289,991	7,831,219	1,120,539	10,369	3,788,679	25,394	7,825,290	78,826	1,290,162	32,624,853

* Juniper Woodlands and Rocky Mountain Juniper discussions are combined in the report.

** In the report, there are separate discussions for the Douglas-fir forest type west of the Cascade Mountain Range (Coastal Douglas-fir) and the Douglas-fir forest type east of the Cascades (Non-coastal Douglas-fir).

*** Numbers may not add due to rounding.

Pinyon/Juniper Woodlands

Nearly 50 percent of the forest land managed by the BLM outside of Alaska (just over 16 million acres) consists of pinyon/juniper woodlands where a mix of pinyon and juniper species predominate, although some stands of pure or nearly pure pinyon are assigned to this forest type. Stands with juniper and no stocking in pinyon are assigned to either general juniper types (i.e., juniper woodland) or specific juniper types (i.e., Western juniper and Rocky Mountain juniper), although the Rocky Mountain juniper type can have some pinyon stocking.

Pinyon/juniper woodlands on BLM land are dominated by Utah juniper and either singleleaf pinyon (in the western portion of the forest type range) or common (twoneedle) pinyon (in the eastern portion of the forest type range). Other pinyons and junipers found in different areas of the forest type range are Mexican and Arizona pinyon pines, and oneseed, Rocky Mountain, alligator, and California junipers. Together, the pinyons and junipers make up 98 percent of the live trees over 5 inches diameter. Diameter of these species is measured at the root collar (DRC), rather than at breast height (DBH). Broadleaf species, most often low-stature species, also occur as a minor component of pinyon/juniper woodlands, accounting for 1.6 percent of live trees over 5 inches diameter. The most frequent of these are curlleaf mountain-mahogany and Gambel oak. The remaining 0.4 percent of live trees over 5 inches diameter that occur in pinyon/juniper woodland are tall-stature conifers, most commonly Douglas-fir and ponderosa pine.

Pinyon/juniper woodlands range in elevation from just less than 4,000 feet in Utah to just over 9,000 feet in Colorado. The type occurs in eight States, and is the most common forest type in six of those States. (Table 2-1 shows the estimated acreage of pinyon/juniper woodland on BLM land by State.)

The average pinyon/juniper woodland stand has 218 live trees 1-inch diameter and greater per acre. About 31 percent of stands have less than 100 trees per acre, and 27 percent have 300 or more trees per acre.

Figure PJ 1 displays the area of pinyon/juniper woodland by trees-per-acre class.

Figure PJ 2 displays the area of pinyon/juniper woodland by stand-size class. Eighty-two percent of pinyon/juniper stands are in the large-tree stand-size category. The medium-tree and seedling/sapling categories each occupy 5 percent of the area, and 8 percent of the stands are classified as sparse.

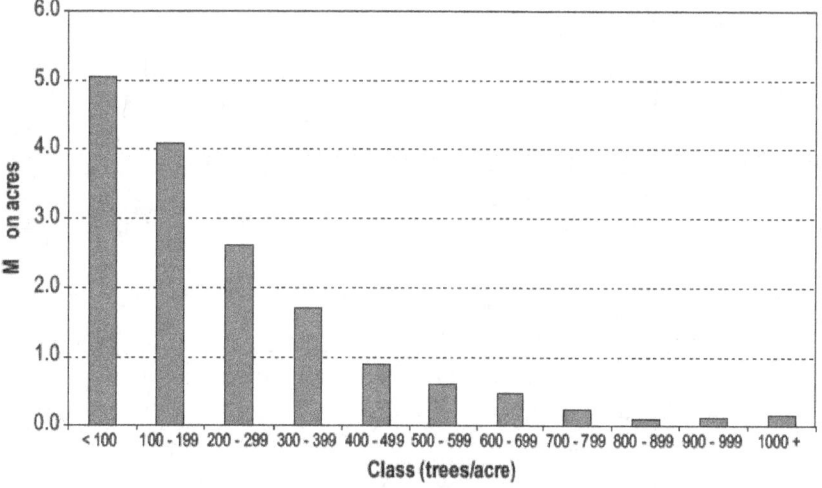

Figure PJ 1 – Area of pinyon/juniper woodland by trees-per-acre class, BLM land.

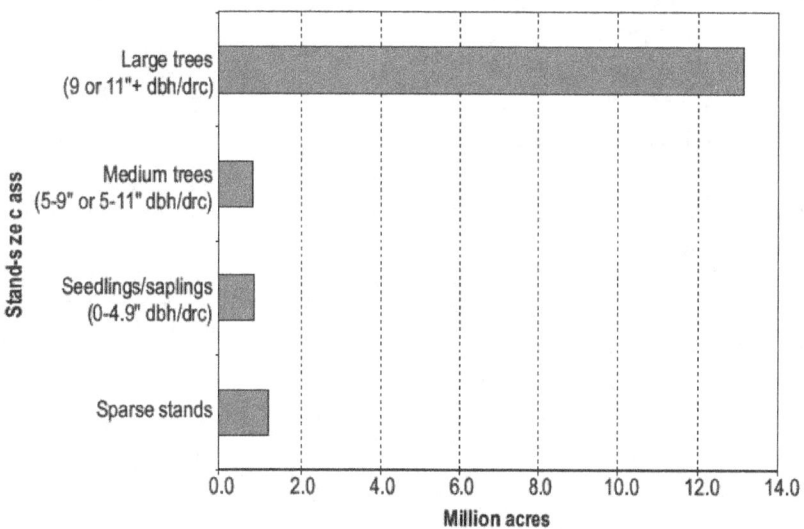

Figure PJ 2 – Area of pinyon/juniper woodland by stand-size class, BLM land.

The area of pinyon/juniper woodland by stand-age class is presented in Figure PJ 3. The most common stand-age class is 151 to 200 years, followed closely by the 101 to 150 year and 51 to 100 year classes. Seventy percent of the area is in stands between 51 and 200 years old.

Pinyon/juniper seldom exists in even-aged stands because pinyon and juniper species tend to accumulate gradually on a site, whether regenerating or encroaching, so stands in any age class often have individual trees that are much older. It may be reasonable to assume that stands that are recently established in otherwise shrub and grassland ecosystems should contain no trees significantly older than the age class. The percentage of the area in the younger age classes that have no recorded live-tree age over 150 years should give an approximation of the degree to which pinyon/juniper stands could be considered encroachment and regeneration since the beginning of European settlement in the West.

At least 55 percent of all stands on BLM land have either a stand age of 151 years or more or contain trees older than 150 years. This would indicate that some trees existed on these sites prior to the interruption of disturbance processes that keep many arid areas in shrub and grass species. These stands could therefore potentially be considered historical woodlands, but may have been less dense in the past. Most of the stands in the remaining 45 percent of the area are potentially encroachment of pinyon/juniper into historical shrub or grasslands, although an unknown portion of them are regeneration of disturbed

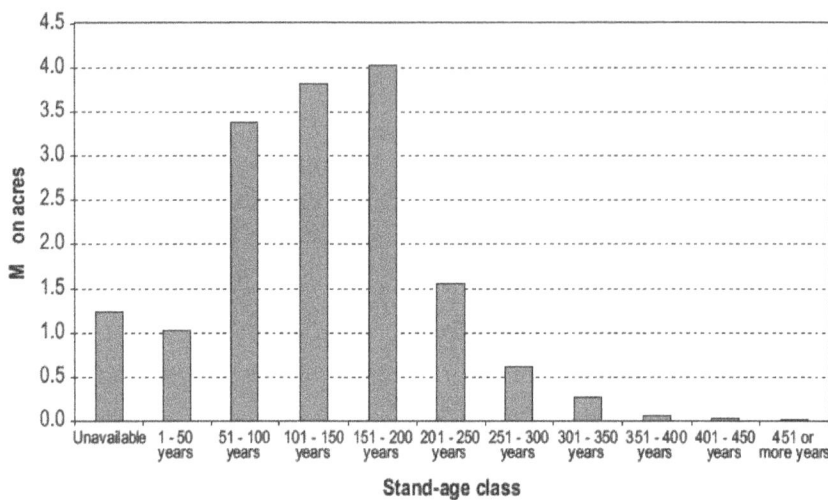

Figure PJ 3 – Area of pinyon/juniper woodland by stand-age class, BLM land.

stands. This portion of the total area of pinyon/juniper woodland represents 77 percent of the area in stand-age classes 150 years and less, or in sparse stands (no stand-age available). About 90 percent of the stands in the age classes 100 years and less and sparse stands have no trees older than 150 years.

Table PJ 1 shows the area by stand-age class and maximum recorded tree age, both divided at 150 years. The reader should realize however, that FIA does not directly measure encroachment by trees into non-forested areas.

Table PJ 2 shows the breakdown of net live volume and live biomass of pinyon/juniper woodland on BLM land by diameter class. In the smaller classes, most of the biomass comes from pinyon species, while junipers are the major contributor to biomass in the large diameter classes. As diameter increases, the contribution from junipers increases, while that from pinyons decreases. Biomass is most evenly distributed between pinyons and junipers in the 13.0 to 14.9 inch class, which is also the class with the maximum values for both biomass and volume.

Table PJ 1. Area (1,000 acres) of pinyon/juniper woodland by stand age and maximum tree age, BLM land.

Stand age	Maximum tree age 150 years or less, or none recorded	Maximum tree age over 150 years
1 – 150 years or unavailable	7,268	2,194 [†]
151 years or more	117 [‡]	6,395

[†] 76 % of this area is in the 101 to 150 years age class.

[‡] Stand age was determined from trees in the plot area that were not included in the plot sample.

Table PJ 2. Net live volume and live biomass on pinyon/juniper woodland, with all pinyons and all junipers live biomass compared, by diameter class, BLM land.

Diameter class (inches)	Volume (million cubic feet)	Biomass (million tons)	Pinyon/Juniper (million tons)†
1.0-2.9	–	2.3	1.4/0.5
3.0-4.9	–	5.3	3.6/1.3
5.0-6.9	445.3	9.1	6.1/2.6
7.0-8.9	723.7	13.5	8.4/4.6
9.0-10.9	985.9	17.6	10.2/6.6
11.0-12.9	1,134.2	19.4	10.5/8.5
13.0-14.9	1,167.2	19.8	9.7/9.5
15.0-16.9	1,044.4	18.0	6.6/10.9
17.0-18.9	868.3	15.0	4.9/9.9
19.0-20.9	680.7	11.6	2.8/8.7
21.0-22.9	493.6	8.7	1.2/7.3
23.0-24.9	406.2	7.3	0.8/6.2
25.0-26.9	313.0	5.5	0.5/5.0
27.0-28.9	230.8	4.0	0.2/3.7
29.0-30.9	243.7	4.0	0.8/3.1
31.0-32.9	114.0	1.9	0.1/1.8
33.0-34.9	83.5	1.4	0.3/1.2
35.0-36.9	33.6	0.6	0.0/0.6
37.0-38.9	36.2	0.6	0.0/0.6
39.0-40.9	30.5	0.5	0.1/0.4
41.0 or more	7.4	0.2	0.0/0.2
Total *	9,042.2	166.1	68.4/93.2

† May not add to total biomass because of biomass from other trees species and rounding.

* Numbers may not add due to rounding.

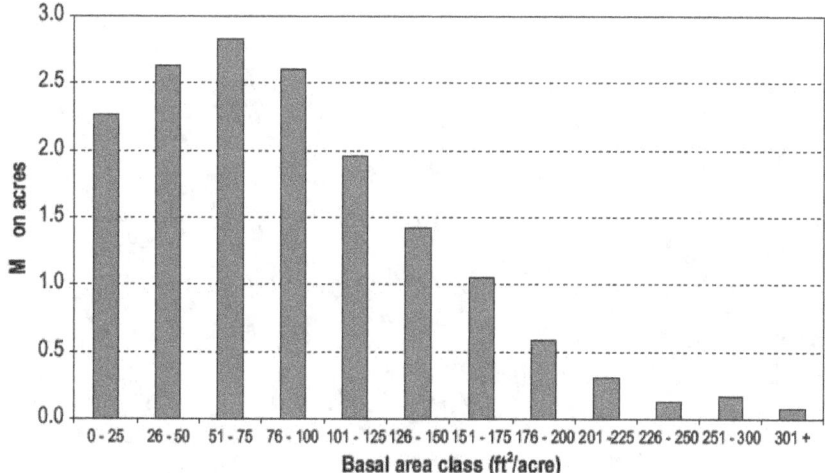

Figure PJ 4. Area of pinyon/juniper woodland by live-tree basal area class, BLM land.

Figure PJ 4 displays the area of pinyon/juniper woodland by basal area class. Fifty-two percent of pinyon/juniper woodland on BLM land is in stands with over 75 square feet per acre. The average is 86 square feet per acre of live tree basal area.

The distribution of SDI, as a percent of the **maximum SDI (SDI_{max})** for pinyon/juniper, is shown in Figure PJ 5. Fifty-two percent of stands have an SDI of at least 35 percent SDI_{max}, and so are considered to be fully occupied. Most stands fall in the SDI classes of either less than 25 percent SDI_{max} (densities below the onset of competition) or between 35 and 60 percent SDI_{max} (fully occupied, but not yet self-thinning). At least 21 percent are over 60 percent SDI_{max}, and are influenced by the onset of self-thinning mortality.

There are 194 million snags, 5.0 inches diameter and greater on BLM pinyon/juniper woodland, for an average of 12.1 per acre. The majority of these snags are from Utah juniper at 46 percent, singleleaf pinyon at 27 percent, and common pinyon at 21 percent. These proportions are nearly the same as the species' percentages of live trees 5.0 inches diameter and greater (Utah juniper at 45 percent, singleleaf pinyon at 27 percent, and common pinyon at 23 percent). Larger snags at least 11 inches diameter occur at an average density of 4.6 per acre. There are an estimated 0.6 very large (19 inches diameter and greater) snags per acre on pinyon/juniper woodland. About 77 percent of these very large snags are from Utah juniper. Figure PJ 6 shows the distribution of snags in these three diameter classes.

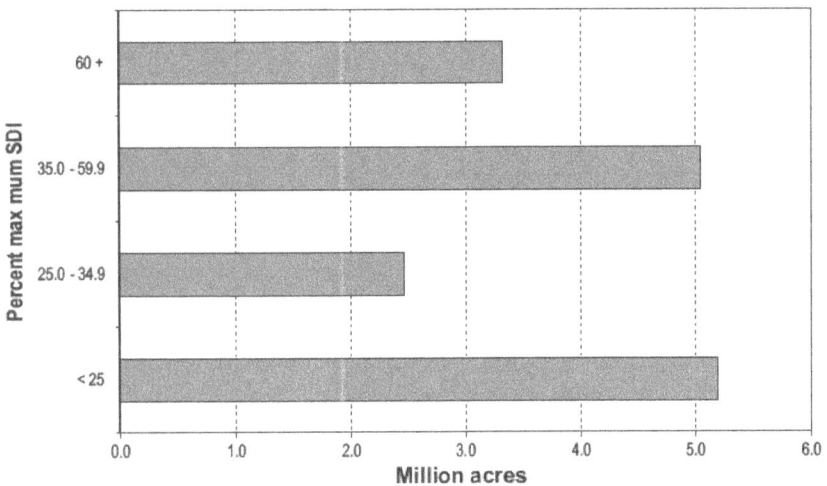

Figure PJ 5 – Area of pinyon/juniper woodland by percent of maximum stand density index (SDI), BLM land.

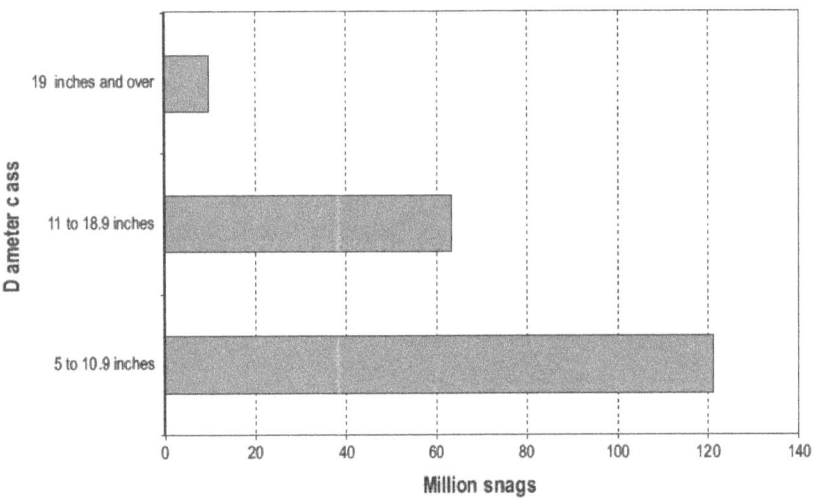

Figure PJ 6 – Number of standing dead trees (snags) on pinyon/ juniper woodlands by diameter class, BLM land.

Combined Juniper Woodlands

Two juniper species in the Western United States (Rocky Mountain and western juniper) are considered by FIA as ecologically or commercially distinctive enough to be assigned specific forest types; stands of other junipers are designated "juniper woodland." These two distinct types are among the 10 most common on BLM forest land. Western juniper is distinguished by the tall stature of the trees and is discussed later in this report as "western juniper forests." Rocky Mountain juniper is less distinct from other junipers. In the IW-FIA periodic inventories, stands with a plurality of stocking in Rocky Mountain juniper were classified as juniper woodland. Since the data from Wyoming and New Mexico for this report comes from periodic data, much of the juniper woodland in those States will likely be classified as Rocky Mountain juniper when the annual inventory begins. For clarity, we will combine juniper woodland and Rocky Mountain juniper woodland types and refer to them as "combined juniper woodland."

Combined juniper woodlands cover almost 19 percent of BLM forest land (totaling 6.2 million acres). The combined forest type is most often dominated by Utah juniper, which comprises 80 percent of the live trees over 5 inches diameter, and is found in every State that has these woodlands. All of the other juniper species comprise the plurality of trees on at least some stands within their ranges. They include Rocky Mountain, California, oneseed, redberry,

and alligator juniper. Rocky Mountain juniper occurs in the northern parts of the woodland range, and the others are more southern species. Over 95 percent of live trees over 5 inches diameter belong to a juniper species. Low-stature broadleaf species, primarily Gambel oak and curlleaf mountain-mahogany make up 1 percent of the live trees over 5 inches diameter. Two percent of the trees are common pinyon, and these all come from stands classified as Rocky Mountain juniper woodland in States with annual inventories. Tall-stature conifers make up another 2 percent; most often, these are ponderosa pine and/or Douglas-fir.

Combined juniper woodlands average about 130 live trees per acre at least 1 inch diameter, with 61 percent of the stands having less than 100 trees per acre and 18 percent of stands having over 200 trees per acre. Figure CJW 1 shows the distribution of juniper woodland area by trees-per-acre class. Combined juniper woodland is the most widely distributed forest type on a State basis. It occurs on BLM land in 10 States and is found at elevations ranging from 1,500 feet in California to

8,300 feet in New Mexico. (Table 2-1 shows the estimated acreage of combined juniper woodland, separated between juniper woodland and Rocky Mountain juniper woodland, on BLM land by State.)

Figure CJW 2 displays the area of combined juniper woodland by stand-size class. Seventy-nine percent of the area is in the large-tree stand-size class, with nearly 17 percent in sparse stands. Three percent of the stands are in the seedling/sapling class, and 2 percent are in the medium tree stand-size class.

Figure CJW 3 displays the distribution of combined juniper woodland area by stand-age class. The three most common classes, from 51 to 200 years, have a fairly even distribution among them at a little over 1.3 million acres each. Collectively, they make up 65 percent of the area. Stands with no age available are also very common in combined juniper woodlands, primarily due to the large acreage of sparse stands. Seventeen percent of the stands are in the "unavailable" stand-age class.

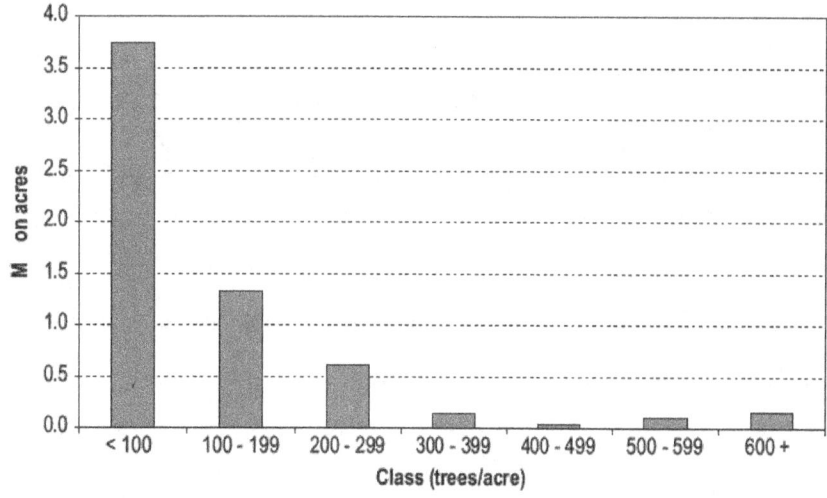

Figure CJW 1 – Area of combined juniper woodland by trees-per-acre class, BLM land.

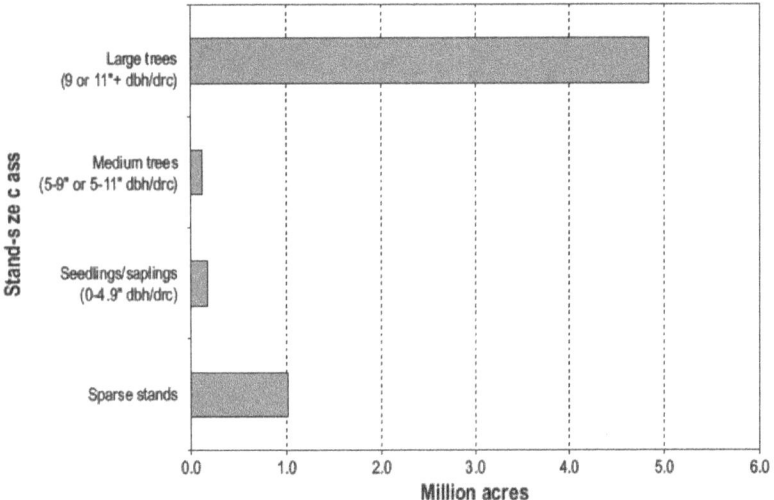

Figure CJW 2 – Area of combined juniper woodland by stand-size class, BLM land.

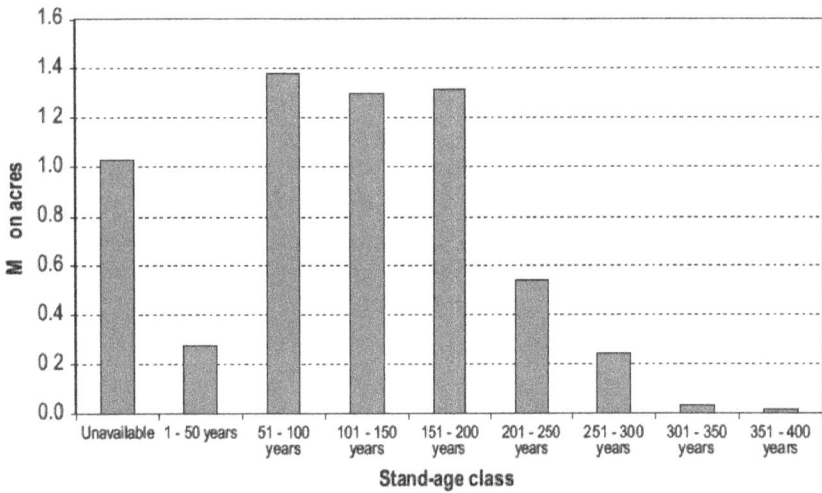

Figure CJW 3 – Area of combined juniper woodland by stand-age class, BLM land.

Table CJW 1. Area (1000 acres) of combined juniper woodland by stand age and maximum tree age, BLM land.

Stand age	Maximum tree age 150 years or less, or none recorded	Maximum tree age over 150 years
1 - 150 years or unavailable	3,628	365 †
151 years or more	106 ‡	2,054

† 68 % of this area is in the 101 to 150 years age class.

‡ Stand age was determined from trees in the plot area that were not included in the plot sample.

Similar to pinyon/juniper, the combined juniper woodlands usually establish very slowly in an area over a long period of time, so these woodlands are usually uneven-aged. Table CJW 1 shows the area of combined juniper woodlands by stand-age class and the maximum recorded live-tree age, both with a cutoff of 150 years. Only 41 percent of the stands either have a stand age of over 150 years or live trees on the stand older than 150 years, indicating historical stands. This means that 59 percent of the stands are likely to be either encroachment into historical shrub or grassland by junipers, or regeneration of disturbed stands. This represents about 91 percent of the area in stands with age classes less than 150 years or unavailable. The reader should realize however, that FIA does not directly measure encroachment by trees into non-forested areas.

The volume and biomass on BLM combined juniper woodlands, broken down by diameter class, is shown in Table CJW 2. The maximum values for volume and biomass are found in the 15.0 to 16.9 inch class. Utah juniper contributes 77 percent of the biomass, and juniper species as a whole contain 93 percent of the biomass. Biomass in the larger classes tends to come from Utah juniper, Rocky Mountain juniper, California juniper, and ponderosa pine. The largest contribution to biomass other than junipers is ponderosa pine at 2.4 percent.

Table CJW 2. Net live volume and live biomass on combined juniper woodland by diameter class, BLM land.

Diameter class (inches)	Volume (million cubic feet)	Biomass (million tons)
1.0-2.9	--	0.4
3.0-4.9	--	0.8
5.0-6.9	63.1	1.4
7.0-8.9	112.6	2.3
9.0-10.9	165.2	3.3
11.0-12.9	211.4	4.0
13.0-14.9	251.8	4.6
15.0-16.9	271.4	5.1
17.0-18.9	232.0	4.3
19.0-20.9	224.4	4.2
21.0-22.9	172.0	3.1
23.0-24.9	124.4	2.3
25.0-26.9	107.3	1.9
27.0-28.9	73.3	1.3
29.0-30.9	66.9	1.2
31.0-32.9	35.7	0.6
33.0-34.9	36.3	0.6
35.0-36.9	18.0	0.3
37.0-38.9	10.1	0.2
39.0-40.9	16.8	0.3
41.0 or more	21.0	0.3
Total *	2,213.7	42.5

* Numbers may not add due to rounding

Figure CJW 4 displays the area of combined juniper woodland by basal area class. It indicates that only 32 percent of combined juniper woodlands on BLM land are in stands with over 75 square feet per acre. The average is 65 square feet per acre of live tree basal area. The distribution of combined juniper woodland area by percent of SDImax is shown in Figure CJW 5. Most combined juniper woodland stands, 58 percent, are at less than 25 percent SDImax, or the onset of competition. Thirty-one percent of the juniper woodland acreage is in stands that are considered to be fully occupied, or at least 35 percent SDImax.

Snags of 5 inches diameter and greater occur on combined juniper woodland at an average of 7.7 per acre. There are about 47 million snags of this size on BLM combined juniper woodlands. There are an estimated 3.0 large snags per acre (11 inches diameter and greater) and 0.4 very large snags per acre (at least 19 inches diameter). All of the snags recorded in the very large category were juniper species, and 78 percent were Utah junipers. Figure CJW 6 shows the distribution of snags in these three size classes.

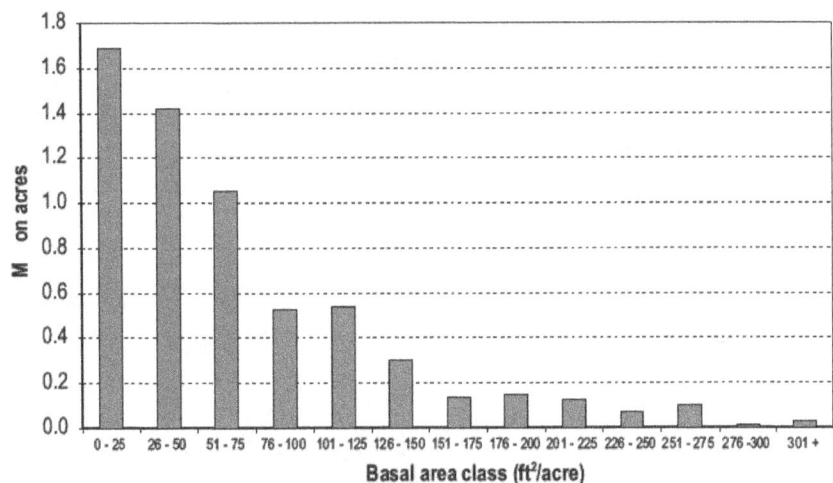

Figure CJW 4 – Area of combined juniper woodland by live-tree basal area class, BLM land.

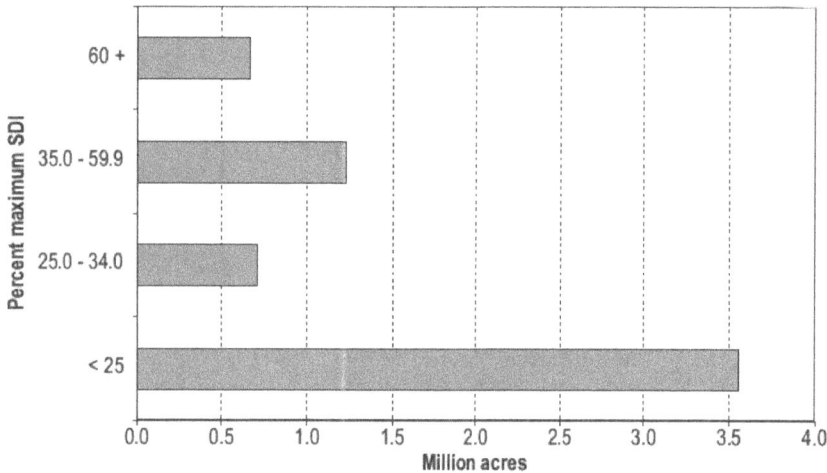

Figure CJW 5 – Area of combined juniper woodland by percent of maximum stand density index (SDI), BLM land.

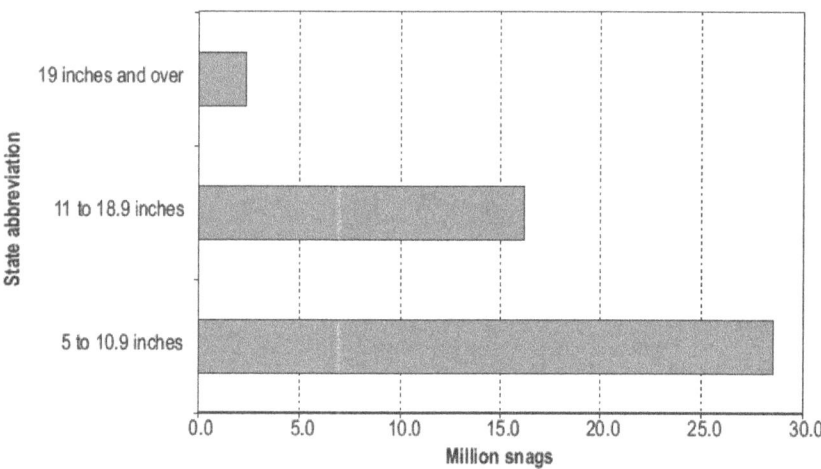

Figure CJW 6 – Number of standing dead trees (snags) on combined juniper woodlands by size, BLM land.

Douglas-fir Forests

Douglas-fir forests are found in eight States (see Table 2-1). They cover 2.7 million acres on BLM land, making them the third most common forest type at 8 percent of BLM forest land. Douglas-fir is a very adaptable and widespread species, occurring in several ecological regions across its range, from coastal rainforests in the northwest to arid environments in the intermountain west. While there is some debate as to how the Douglas-fir subspecies or variants should be discussed separately, FIA considers Douglas-fir to be a single species. (Bigcone Douglas-fir is a separate species, occurring only in California. It has not yet been encountered on any plots on BLM land.)

The BLM requested that the Douglas fir data analysis be separated by the Cascade Mountain Range in Oregon. West of the Cascades, the climate is much wetter than on the east side; some areas are classified as temperate rainforest. Also, the most productive and most intensely managed forests administered by the BLM are in western Oregon. Over 70 percent of the forests west of the Cascades are Douglas-fir forests. Because these forests are so important to the BLM, and because they occur in a much wetter moisture regime, this report will treat coastal Douglas-fir forests (west of the Cascades) separately from non-coastal Douglas-fir forests (east of the Cascades) on BLM lands.

Coastal Douglas-fir Forests

Of the 2.7 million acres of Douglas-fir on BLM land, 1.5 million acres occur in 19 coastal counties in Oregon and in coastal northern California (17,000 acres). Sixty-nine percent of the live trees at least 5 inches diameter are Douglas-firs, with all of the combined conifer species making up 84 percent. The most common of these, other than Douglas-fir, is western hemlock at 9 percent of the live trees 5 inches diameter and greater. The remaining 16 percent of the trees are broadleaf species, with Pacific madrone and bigleaf maple being the most common. Comparing tree species using total live basal area (5 inches diameter and greater), which focuses on the larger trees in a forest stand, 78 percent is in Douglas-firs, 92 percent is in combined conifers, and the remaining 8 percent is in broadleaf species.

Coastal Douglas-fir forests range in elevation from 300 to 4,700 feet, occurring most commonly between 1,000 and 1,900 feet. The stands average 307 trees per acre (live trees at least 1 inch diameter), with 12 percent of the area having less than 100 trees per acre, and 21 percent having over 400 trees per acre. Figure C-DF 1 shows the area of coastal Douglas-fir forests by trees-per-acre class.

Eighty-one percent of the Douglas-fir forest area west of the Cascades is in the large-tree stand-size class. Fifteen percent of the stands are stocked with medium-size trees, and 4 percent are in the seedling/sapling size class. No stands of coastal Douglas-fir forest were classified as sparse stands (or "nonstocked"). Figure C-DF 2 shows the area of coastal Douglas-fir forest by stand-size class.

The area of coastal Douglas-fir forests by stand-age class is presented in Figure C-DF 3. The largest portion of the acreage is in the 1 to 50 year class, followed by the 51 to 100 year, then the 101 to 150 year classes. Eighty-four percent of the area is between 1 and 150 years old. Fifty-eight percent of the area in the 1 to 50 year stand age is also in the large-tree stand-size class, indicating the growth rate of trees in coastal Douglas-fir stands. The high proportion of young stands, even though no stands were classified as sparse, is an indication of the favorable

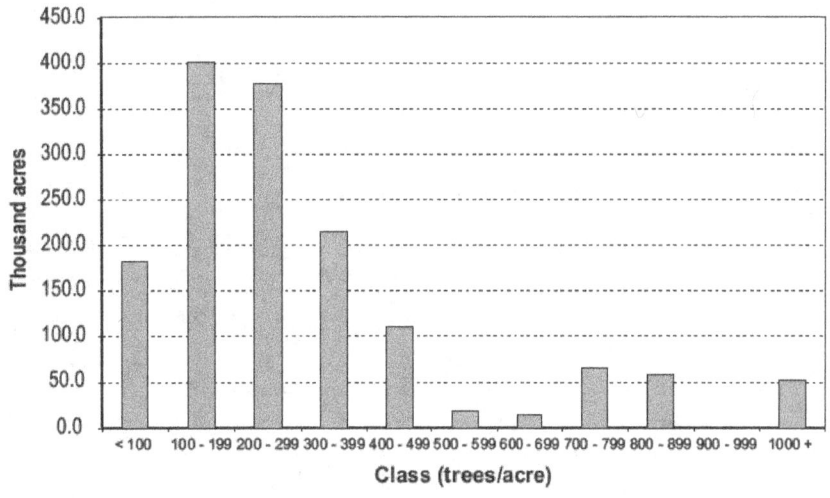

Figure C-DF 1 – Area of coastal douglas-fir forest by trees-per-acre class, BLM land.

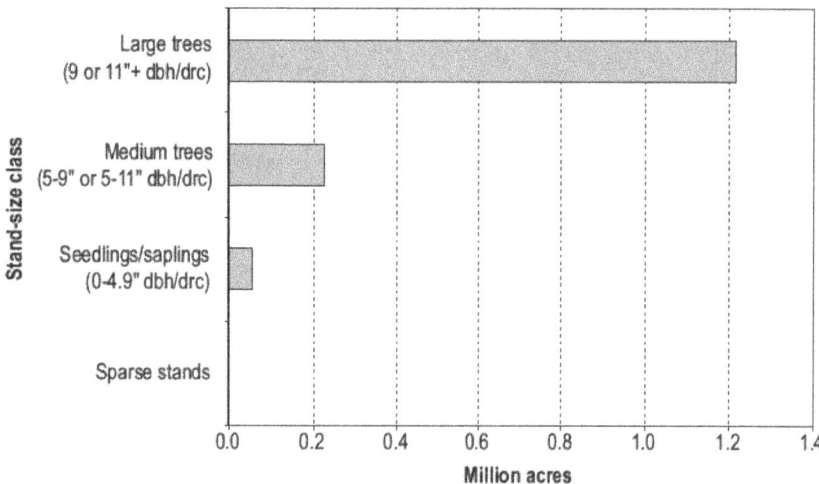

Figure C-DF 2 – Area of coastal douglas-fir forest by stand-size class, BLM land.

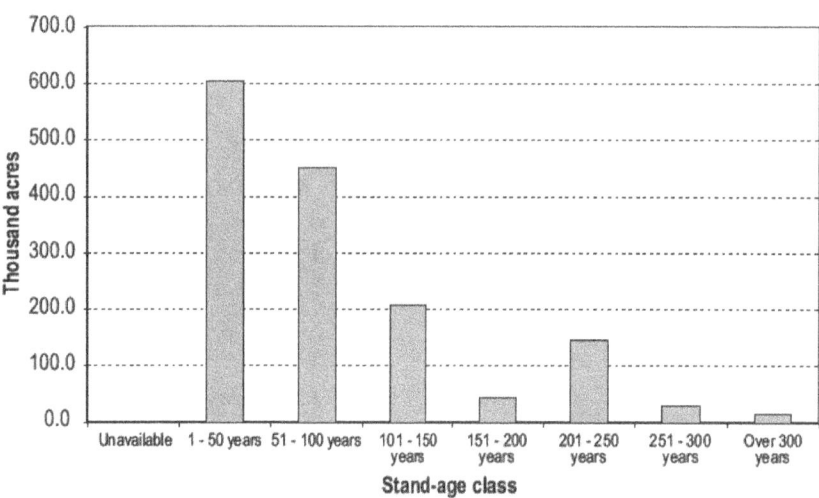

Figure C-DF 3 – Area of coastal douglas-fir forest by stand-age class, BLM land.

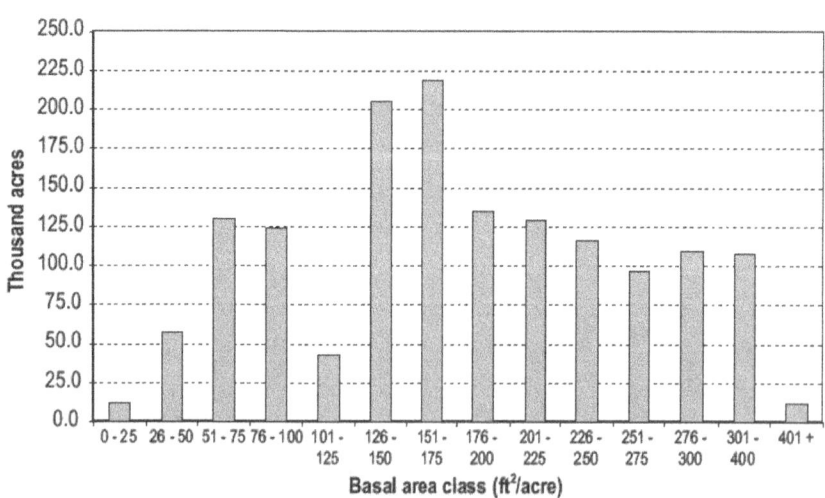

Figure C-DF 4 – Area of coastal douglas-fir forest by live-tree basal class, BLM land.

conditions and active management (including tree planting) that lead to rapid reforestation after disturbance. Trees were available for aging on all of the plots, so none were assigned to the age class "unavailable."

Volume and biomass for coastal Douglas-fir forest are listed by diameter class in Table C-DF 1. The large number of diameter classes is an indication of how large trees can grow in coastal areas. Also, volume and biomass are higher than either pinyon/juniper or juniper woodlands, even though the area covered by coastal Douglas-fir forest is substantially less. This is an indication of how much more wood fiber is found in moist forests than in arid woodlands. Eighty-two percent of the volume comes from Douglas-fir trees, with the next-largest volume contributor being western hemlock at 6.6 percent. Douglas-fir trees were the only species with a measured diameter of 55.0 inches or more. Other species contributing wood volume from large trees 45.0 inches to 54.9 inches are incense-cedar, sugar pine, and ponderosa pine.

Eighty-seven percent of coastal Douglas-fir forest area has over 75 square feet per acre of live tree basal area. Figure C-DF 4 shows how the area is distributed over basal area classes. The average is 181 square feet per acre of basal area in live trees. These numbers show that these forest stands tend to be very dense (many trees), or have very large trees, sometimes both.

The distribution of area by SDI as a percent of the SDI_{max} is shown for coastal Douglas-fir in Figure C-DF 5. Eighty-five percent

Table C-DF 1. Net live volume and live biomass on coastal Douglas-fir forests by diameter class, BLM land.

Diameter class (inches)	Volume (million cubic feet)	Biomass (million tons)
1.0-2.9	–	0.8
3.0-4.9	–	1.7
5.0-6.9	194.8	5.3
7.0-8.9	374.8	8.0
9.0-10.9	561.9	11.1
11.0-12.9	517.6	9.7
13.0-14.9	607.0	11.2
15.0-16.9	599.6	11.1
17.0-18.9	478.8	8.9
19.0-20.9	629.7	11.8
21.0-22.9	406.2	7.4
23.0-24.9	515.8	9.7
25.0-26.9	338.0	6.7
27.0-28.9	298.9	6.3
29.0-30.9	300.9	5.6
31.0-32.9	317.3	6.4
33.0-34.9	373.9	7.1
35.0-36.9	359.2	7.2
37.0-38.9	326.2	6.8
39.0-40.9	231.4	4.7
41.0-42.9	261.4	5.2
43.0-44.9	287.7	5.9
45.0-46.9	148.0	2.9
47.0-48.9	251.8	4.9
49.0-50.9	247.8	5.0
51.0-52.9	120.6	2.5
53.0-54.9	136.7	2.7
55.0-56.9	108.0	2.3
57.0-58.9	24.0	0.5
59.0-60.9	12.7	0.2
61.0 or more	192.9	3.9
Total *	**9,223.3**	**183.7**

* Numbers may not add due to rounding

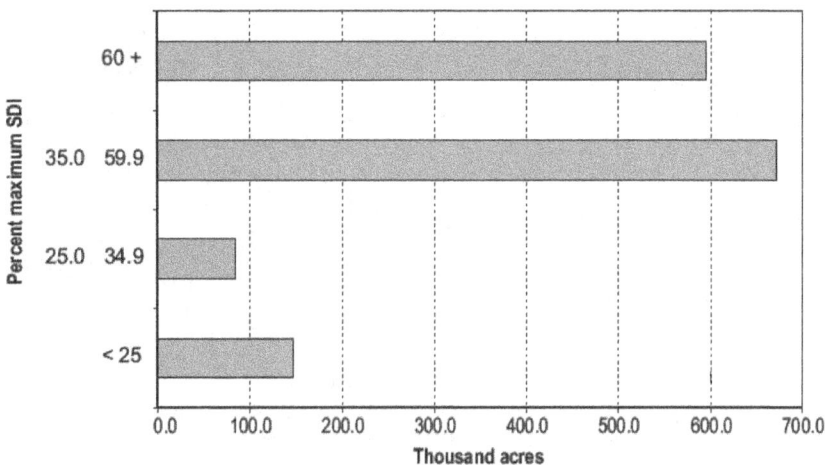

Figure C-DF 5 – Area of coastal douglas-fir forest by percent of maximum stand density index (SDI), BLM land.

of the area is in stands with at least 35 percent SDI$_{max}$, or fully occupied. Forty percent of the stands are fully stocked but not at self-thinning densities (between 35 and 60 percent SDI$_{max}$), and 10 percent are at low densities without competition between trees (less than 25 percent SDI$_{max}$). Again, this indicates that most stands have some combination of many trees and/or very large trees.

About 25 million snags, 5.0 inches diameter and greater, are found on coastal Douglas-fir forests for a density of 16.7 per acre. The average density for Douglas-fir forests across all land ownerships in the Western United States is 21.7 snags per acre. Large snags (11 inches diameter or over) occur at a density of 5.6 snags per acre, and very large snags (at least 19 inches diameter) at 2.2 snags per acre. The distribution of snags in these size classes is shown in Figure C-DF 6. Snags from Douglas-fir trees make up 62 percent of all the snags over 5 inches diameter, 77 percent of all large snags, and 86 percent of very large snags. Other species commonly found as very large snags 19 inches diameter and more are ponderosa pine with 5 percent and California black oak and Pacific madrone with nearly 3 percent each.

The BLM is currently in a major land use planning effort in Western Oregon, which includes most of the Coastal Douglas-fir forest type. The inventories to support this planning effort are of a different design, so that data may vary substantially from the numbers in this report.

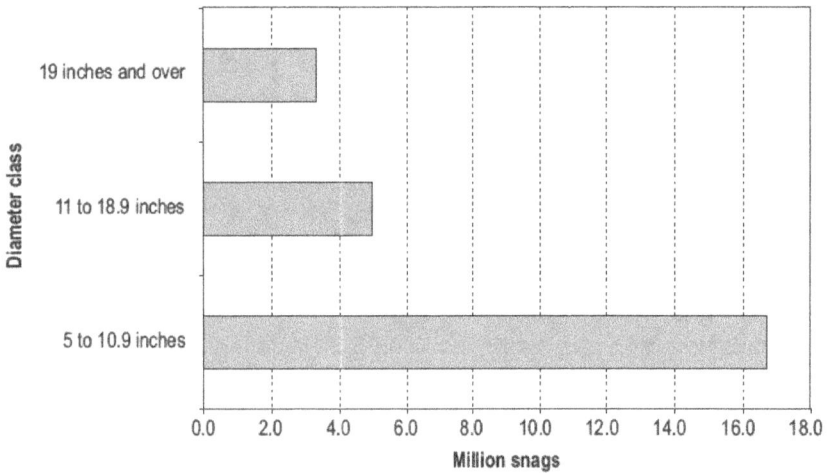

Figure C-DF 6 – Number of standing dead trees (snags) on coastal douglas-fir forests by diameter class, BLM land.

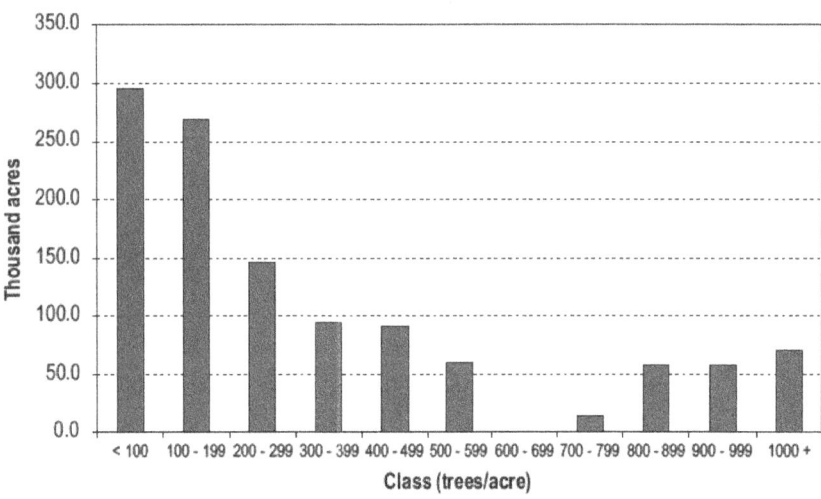

Figure NC-DF 1 – Area of non-coastal douglas-fir forest by trees-per-acre class, BLM land.

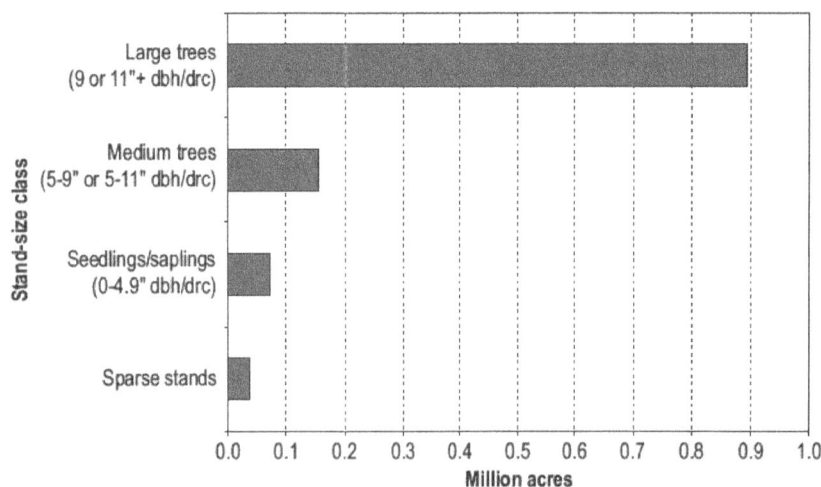

Figure NC-DF 2 – Area of non-coastal douglas-fir forest by stand-size class, BLM land.

Non-coastal Douglas-fir Forests

Forty-four percent of Douglas-fir forests on BLM lands, or 1.2 million acres, occurs in non-coastal areas in seven States, including 62,494 acres in Washington and Oregon east of the Cascade Range (see Table 2-1 for State acreages). Douglas-fir make up 76 percent of the live trees at least 5 inches diameter in this forest type, and all of the combined conifers, including Douglas-fir make up 97 percent of live trees. The most common other conifer in non-coastal Douglas-fir stands is ponderosa pine at 4 percent of the trees, and limber pine, Rocky Mountain juniper, lodgepole pine, and subalpine fir each contribute between 2 and 3 percent. Three species of broadleaf trees, quaking aspen, curlleaf mountain mahogany, and Gambel oak, comprise 3 percent of the live trees 5 inches diameter or more, with quaking aspen by far the most common. Comparing live trees at least 5 inches diameter by total live basal area, Douglas-firs contribute 81 percent, all conifers 99 percent, and broadleaf trees 1 percent.

Non-coastal Douglas-fir forests are found at elevations ranging from 2,200 feet in Idaho (Montana also has stands at less than 3,000 feet) to 9,900 feet in Colorado (Utah also has stands at over 9,000 feet). The average stand has 376 live trees per acre. Figure NC-DF 1 shows the distribution of non-coastal Douglas-fir forests by trees-per-acre class, with 26 percent of the area at less than 100 live trees per acre and 23 percent at over 500 live trees per acre.

Figure NC-DF 2 displays the distribution of stand-size classes of non-coastal Douglas-fir forest, with 77 percent of the area in the large-tree stand-size class. Thirteen percent of the area is in the medium-tree size class, 6 percent in the seedling/sapling size, and 3 percent classified as sparse stands.

Non-coastal Douglas-fir forest stands are, on average, a little older than coastal stands; the 51 to 100 year stand-age class is the most common. The oldest recorded stand, however, is 269 years old, compared to 420 years old for the oldest coastal stand. Figure NC-DF 3 shows the area of non-coastal Douglas-fir forests by stand-age class.

Net live wood volume and live biomass are shown by diameter class in Table NC-DF 1. The largest diameter class shown is 39 inches or more (the maximum measured diameter was 45.0 inches), substantially less than the large number of diameter classes shown in table C-DF1 for coastal Douglas-fir, where the largest diameter class was 61 inches or more (maximum diameter was 88.9 inches). Douglas-fir trees generally contribute larger proportions of the volume in larger diameter classes, making up 66 percent of the volume in the 5.0 to 6.9 class and 88 percent of all classes 19.0 inches or more. Other species contributing significant volume to the larger classes (19.0 or more) are lodgepole pine and ponderosa pine, each making up almost 3 percent of the volume in these classes.

The distribution of live basal area per acre on non-coastal Douglas-fir forests is shown in Figure NC-DF 4. Fifty-nine percent of the area has over 75 square

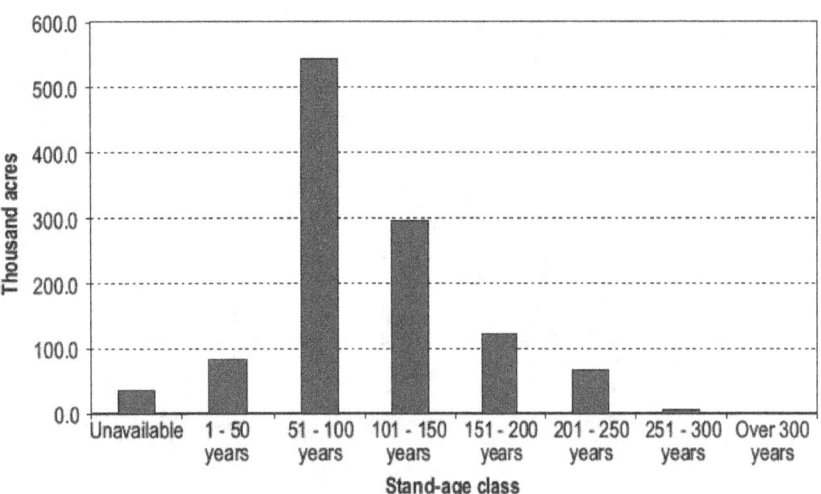

Figure NC-DF 3 – Area of non-coastal douglas-fir forest by stand-age class, BLM land.

Table NC-DF 1. Net live volume and live biomass on non-coastal Douglas-fir forests by diameter class, BLM land.

Diameter class (inches)	Volume (million cubic feet)	Biomass (million tons)
1.0-2.9	--	0.8
3.0-4.9	--	2.3
5.0-6.9	115.4	2.8
7.0-8.9	200.0	4.3
9.0-10.9	238.5	4.8
11.0-12.9	233.2	4.5
13.0-14.9	258.7	5.0
15.0-16.9	224.0	4.4
17.0-18.9	165.1	3.2
19.0-20.9	172.9	3.3
21.0-22.9	90.1	1.7
23.0-24.9	25.3	0.5
25.0-26.9	52.5	1.0
27.0-28.9	75.2	1.4
29.0-30.9	34.8	0.7
31.0-32.9	3.8	0.1
33.0-34.9	0.0	0.0
35.0-36.9	2.9	0.1
37.0-38.9	2.2	†
39.0 or more	4.2	0.1
Total *	**1,898.9**	**41.1**

† Less than 50,000. Entries showing "0.0" had no measured trees in that diameter class.

* Numbers may not add due to rounding

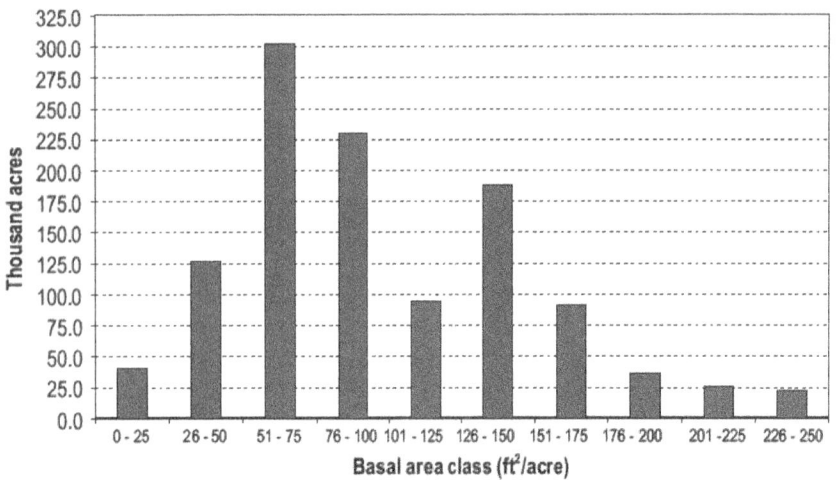

Figure NC-DF 4 – Area of non-coastal douglas-fir forest by live-tree basal area class, BLM land.

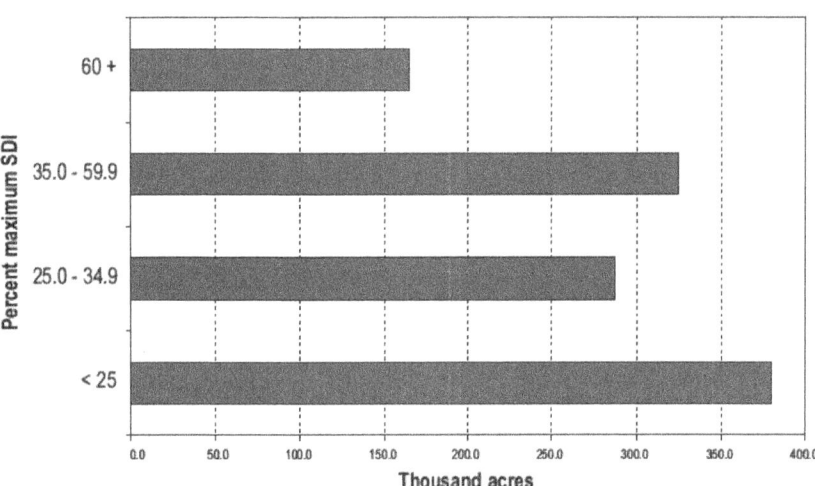

Figure NC-DF 5 – Area of non-coastal douglas-fir forest by percent of maximum stand density index (SDI), BLM land.

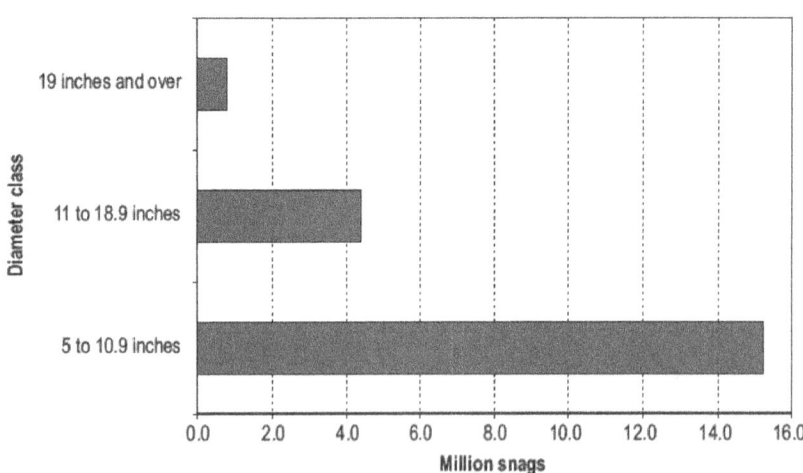

Figure NC-DF 6 – Number of standing dead trees (snags) on non-coastal douglas-fir forests by diameter class, BLM land.

feet of live basal area per acre, with the average stand having 96 square feet per acre. While these numbers are somewhat higher than the woodland discusses so far, they are much less than those for coastal Douglas-fir.

Forty-two percent of the acreage of non-coastal Douglas-fir forests is considered to be fully occupied, as shown by an SDI of more than 35 percent of the SDImax. Figure NC-DF 5 shows how the area is distributed by percent SDImax. The largest proportion of the stands, 33 percent, is sparse enough that competition between individual trees has not yet begun (less than 25 percent SDImax). Twenty-eight percent of the area is at full occupancy, but not yet at the stage of mortality-related self thinning (35 to 60 percent SDImax). Twenty-five percent of the area is in stands experiencing competition between trees, but not yet fully occupied (25 to 34.9 percent SDImax), and 14 percent is undergoing self thinning (over 60 percent SDImax).

About 20.4 million snags, 5 inches diameter or greater, are found on non-coastal Douglas-fir forests, with an average density of 17.6 snags per acre. Larger snags (11 inches diameter or more) occur at an average density of 4.5 per acre, and very large snags (19 inches diameter or more) are present at 0.7 per acre. Figure NC-DF 6 displays the number of snags on non-coastal Douglas-fir forests in these three diameter classes.

Western Juniper Forests

Western juniper is generally considered to be a tall-stature species. The diameters for the species are measured at breast height (unlike the other junipers and other low-stature species). Even though the average height of western junipers is 30 to 40 feet, it is capable of reaching heights of over 80 feet, and normally has a single-stem, erect growth form.

Western juniper forests occur on BLM land in four States, covering 6 percent of the BLM forest land at 1.9 million acres. Ninety-six percent of the live trees over 5 inches diameter found in the western juniper forest type are western juniper trees. The most common species, otherwise, is curlleaf mountain-mahogany at 2 percent. Only six other species were encountered. Western juniper trees were the only tree species found on 90 percent of the western juniper plots.

Western juniper forests are the least dense of the common BLM forest types: eighty-three percent of the western juniper forest area is in stands with less than 100 trees per acre, with an average of 66 trees per acre and a maximum of just over 400 trees per acre. Figure WJ 1 shows the area of western juniper forest by trees per acre (note that area is shown in thousands of acres, rather than millions). Western juniper forests are found at elevations ranging from 1,500 feet in Oregon to 7,500 feet in California. (The estimates for each State's area of western juniper forest are shown in Table 2-1.)

Figure WJ 2 displays the distribution of western juniper forest by stand-size class. The most common stand size is large trees at 54 percent of the forest type area, followed by sparse stands at 30 percent. Fourteen percent of the area is in the seedling/sapling size class, and 2 percent is in the medium-tree size class.

Western juniper forests on BLM land are also relatively young. Figure WJ 3 shows the stand-age class distribution of western juniper forest type area, with the most common being the 51 to 100 year class followed by sparse stands

(unavailable age). The oldest recorded stand age is 300 years.

As with the junipers in woodland forest types, there is some concern with western juniper encroachment into shrub and grasslands. Table WJ 1 shows the area of western juniper forests by age class and the maximum recorded age, both with a cutoff of 150 years.

According to these figures, only 28 percent of the area has a stand age of over 150 or trees on the plot over 150 years, indicating historical stands. The remaining 72 percent represent candidates for

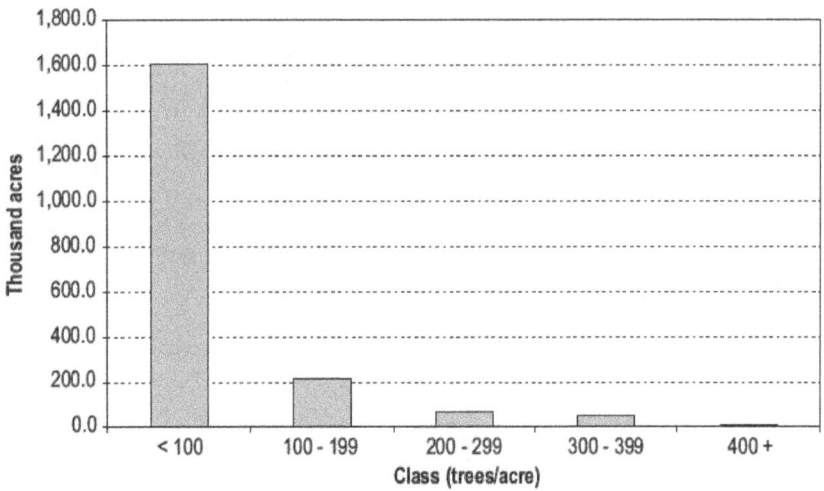

Figure WJ 1 – Area of western juniper forest by trees-per-acre class, BLM land.

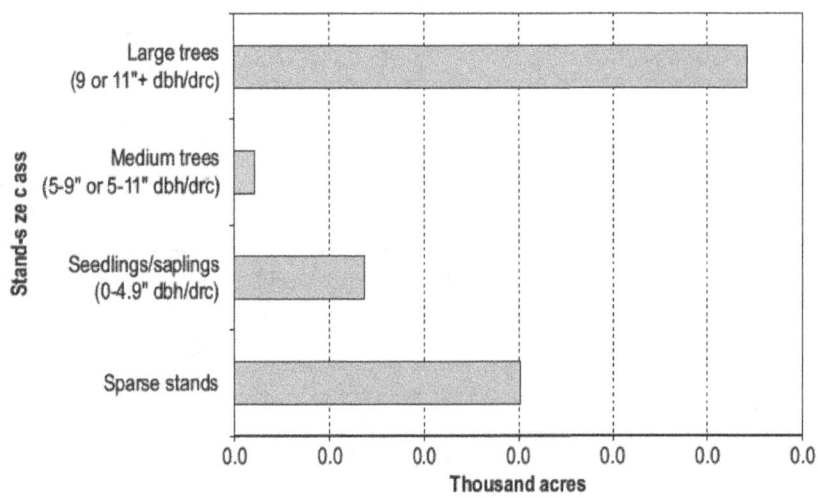

Figure WJ 2 – Area of western juniper forest by stand-size class, BLM land.

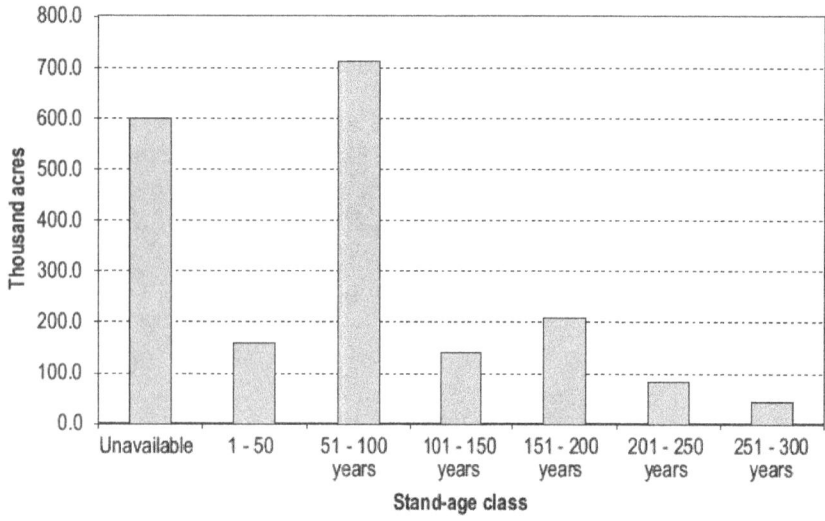

Figure WJ 3 – Area of western juniper forest by stand-age class, BLM land.

Table WJ 1. Area (1000 acres) of western juniper forest by stand age and maximum tree age, BLM land.

Stand age	Maximum tree age 150 years or less, or none recorded	Maximum tree age over 150 years
1 - 150 years or unavailable	1,399	212
151 years or more	160 ‡	176

‡ Stand age was determined from trees in the plot area that were not included in the plot sample.

Table WJ 2. Net live volume and live biomass on western juniper forest by diameter class, BLM land.

Diameter class (inches)	Volume (million cubic feet)	Biomass (million tons)
1.0-2.9	–	0.1
3.0-4.9	–	0.3
5.0-6.9	24.2	0.9
7.0-8.9	39.7	1.2
9.0-10.9	59.2	1.7
11.0-12.9	51.2	1.5
13.0-14.9	37.0	1.0
15.0-16.9	49.9	1.5
17.0-18.9	59.2	1.7
19.0-20.9	22.6	0.7
21.0-22.9	18.1	0.5
23.0-24.9	27.5	0.9
25.0-26.9	12.4	0.4
27.0-28.9	10.6	0.3
29.0-30.9	10.2	0.3
31.0-32.9	2.0	0.1
33.0-34.9	4.6	0.2
35.0-36.9	5.0	0.1
37.0-38.9	1.8	0.1
39.0 or more	0.8	†
Total *	**436.0**	**13.7**

† Less than 50,000

* Numbers may not add due to rounding

encroachment by western juniper. This is not surprising, given that 83 percent of the area has a stand age of 150 years or less. The maximum ages in this case should be taken with some caution, as most of the area is in PNW-FIA States (Oregon and California), and the reported tree ages are at breast height, rather than the calculated total age. The result is that the reported maximum tree ages are younger than actual ages, since it takes a seedling several years to reach breast height. Also, 26 percent of stands had an available stand age, but no individual tree ages, indicating stands that were aged using trees in the plot area that were not included in the sample. The reader should realize however, that FIA does not directly measure encroachment by trees into non-forested areas.

Table WJ 2 shows the net live volume and live biomass of western juniper forest by diameter class. The 17.0 to 18.9 inch class has the most volume and biomass. Ninety-five percent of the volume comes from western juniper trees. The second largest portion comes from ponderosa pine, which makes up nearly 3 percent of the volume even though only 0.14 percent of the live trees over 5 inches diameter are ponderosa pines.

The area of western juniper forest by live basal area class is shown in Figure WJ 4. Only 8 percent of the area is in stands with over 75 square feet per acre of basal area, with an average of 33 square feet per acre.

Nine percent of the area of western juniper forest is considered to be fully occupied, as indicated

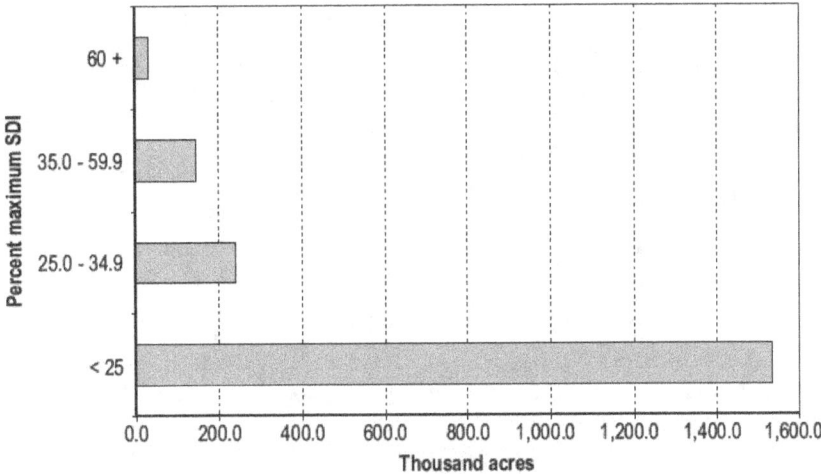

Figure WJ 4 – Area of western juniper forest by live-tree basal area class, BLM land.

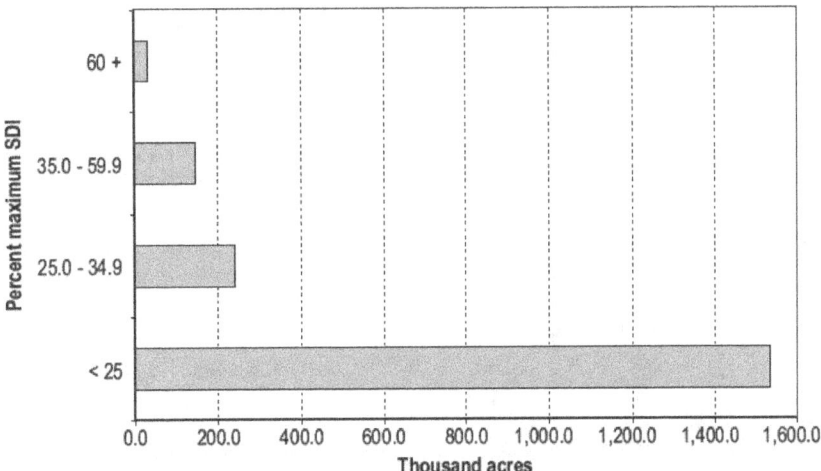

Figure WJ 5 – Area of western juniper forest by live-tree basal area class, BLM land.

by an SDI of over 35 percent of the SDI_{max}. About 7 percent are fully stocked, but not at the point of self thinning (less than 60 percent SDI_{max}), and about 2 percent are fully stocked and influenced by self-thinning.

The area in each percentage of SDI_{max} class is shown in Figure WJ 5. Seventy-nine percent of western juniper forest stands have less than 25 percent SDI_{max} and are not dense enough for competition between individual trees to occur. Twelve percent of the area is at the point of tree competition, but not yet fully occupied (between 25 and 34.9 percent SDI_{max}).

There are 4.9 million snags larger than 5 inches diameter on western juniper forests, or 2.5 snags per acre. Snags over 11 inches diameter are found at 0.9 per acre, and very large snags (over 19 inches diameter) at 0.3 per acre. Figure WJ 6 shows the distribution of snags by these diameter classes. All of the very large snags are western junipers. Over three-quarters of the snags less than 19 inches diameter are also western junipers, and most of the rest are curlleaf mountain mahogany.

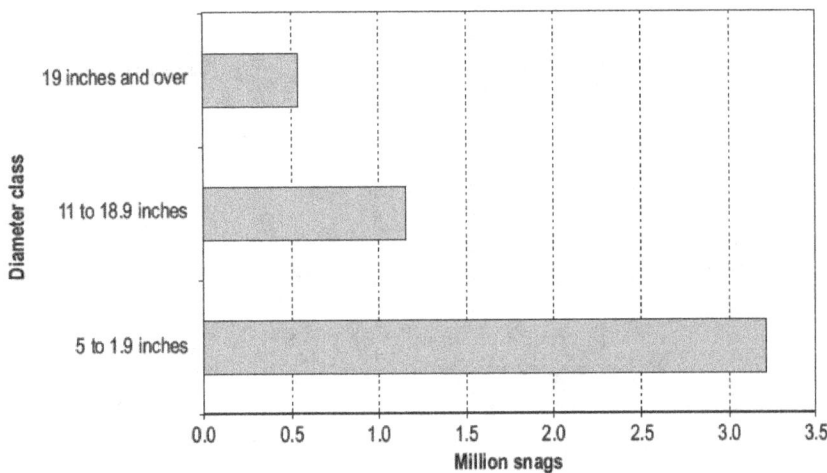

Figure WJ 6 – Number of standing dead trees (snags) on western juniper forests by diameter class, BLM land.

Ponderosa Pine Forests

Just over 1 million acres of ponderosa pine forests are found on BLM land, comprising 3.3 percent of BLM forest land. Found at elevations from 1,700 feet in Oregon to 9,500 feet in Colorado, ponderosa pine forests occur on BLM land in eight States. (The estimated acreages of ponderosa pine forest for each State are listed in Table 2-1.)

Ponderosa pine forests may be considered moderately diverse on BLM land compared to the other common forest types with 27 species found in trees at least 5 inches diameter. Part of the reason for this is that, like Douglas-fir, ponderosa pine occupies a wide range of ecological conditions, including west of the Cascade Range in Oregon. Of the 27 species, 20 are each found in a single State, with 14 occurring only in Oregon—10 west of the Cascades. No other State has more than two unique species. Six of the 10 broadleaf species occurring in ponderosa pine forests are found only in coastal Oregon counties, including the most numerous broadleaf species: Pacific madrone and California black oak. Across the entire range of ponderosa pine forests, 58 percent of live trees 5 inches diameter or more are ponderosa pines, and 93 percent are conifers. The most common of these are Douglas-fir at 14 percent and Rocky Mountain juniper at 11 percent. Ponderosa pine frequently mixes with pinyons and junipers, and 14 percent of the trees are either pinyon or juniper species. The most common of these, Rocky Mountain juniper, common pinyon, and Utah juniper, are each found in several States.

Ponderosa pine forests on BLM land average 262 trees per acre. Figure PP 1 shows the distribution by trees-per-acre class of ponderosa pine forests. Thirty-five percent of the area has less than 100 trees per acre, and 20 percent has over 400 trees per acre. The stands with less than 100 trees per acre include all of the stands with a stand-size of "sparse" (58 percent of stands with less than 100 trees per acre); otherwise, proportions in the large (34 percent), medium (2 percent), and seedling/sapling (6 percent) stand-size classes are similar to those in all stands, with perhaps a few more in the seedling/sapling class and a few less in the large and medium classes. Stands with over 1,000 trees per acre are found in Montana, Oregon, Colorado, and New Mexico, and no State appears to have a disproportionate share of these dense stands.

Seventy percent of the ponderosa pine forest area is in the large-tree stand-size class. Five percent of the stands are stocked with medium-size trees,

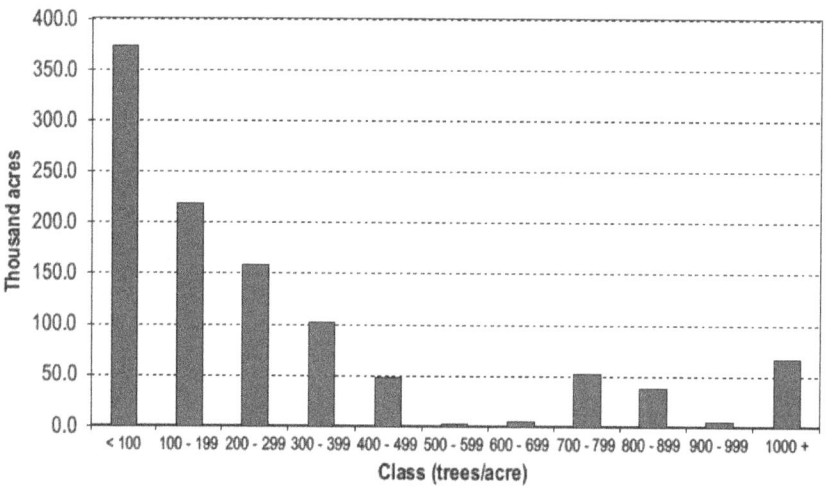

Figure PP 1 – Area of ponderosa pine forest by trees-per-acre class, BLM land.

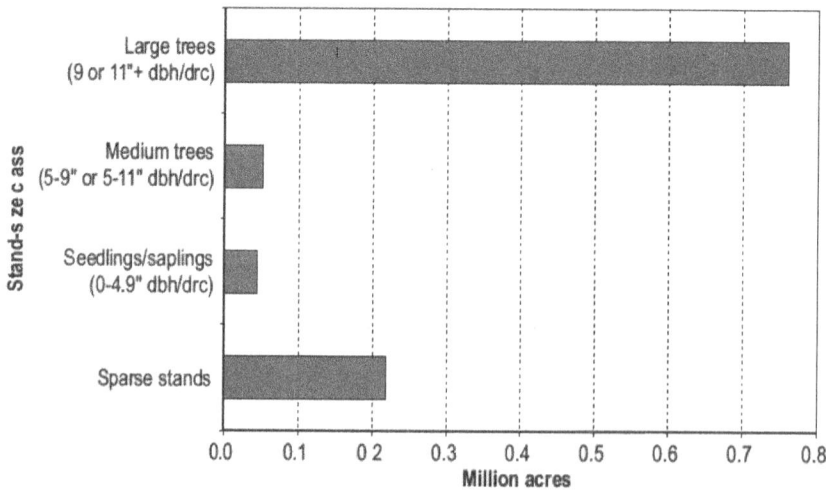

Figure PP 2 – Area of ponderosa pine forest by stand-size class, BLM land.

and another 5 percent are in the seedling/sapling size class. The remaining 20 percent were classified as sparse stands (or "nonstocked"). Figure PP 2 shows the area of ponderosa pine forest by stand-size class.

Ponderosa pine forests on BLM land are relatively young, with the most acreage in the 51 to 100 year age class. The oldest stand sampled was 214 years. The area of ponderosa pine in each age class is shown in Figure PP 3. Two-thirds of the acreage is in stands between 51 and 150 years old.

Ponderosa pine forests on BLM land contain significantly more wood volume per acre than the previously discussed woodland types or western juniper forests, but not nearly as much as Douglas-fir forests. Table PP 1 lists net live volume and live biomass by diameter class. The largest portion of each is in the 13.0 to 14.9 inch class. Sixty-nine percent of the overall net volume comes from ponderosa pine trees, and 18 percent comes from Douglas-fir trees. Nearly three-quarters of the volume from Douglas-firs on ponderosa pine forests is found in coastal Oregon counties. Even though Montana has over two and a half times more area of ponderosa pine forest than coastal Oregon, coastal Oregon's ponderosa pine forests contain almost twice as much net volume as Montana's. Fourteen different tree species contribute to

ponderosa pine forest volume in western Oregon; no other State, including eastern Oregon, has more than seven. Western Oregon's volume also has significant contributions from

Pacific madrone, incense-cedar, California black oak, and sugar pine—species that are found on ponderosa pine forest only in coastal Oregon.

Table PP 1. Net live volume and live biomass on ponderosa pine forest by diameter class, BLM land.

Diameter class (inches)	Volume (million cubic feet)	Biomass (million tons)
1.0-2.9	–	0.5
3.0-4.9	–	1.0
5.0-6.9	61.0	1.7
7.0-8.9	100.5	2.2
9.0-10.9	124.2	2.5
11.0-12.9	140.2	2.7
13.0-14.9	161.3	3.1
15.0-16.9	96.4	1.9
17.0-18.9	107.8	2.2
19.0-20.9	106.0	2.2
21.0-22.9	52.7	1.1
23.0-24.9	36.2	0.8
25.0-26.9	62.7	1.2
27.0-28.9	78.2	1.3
29.0-30.9	45.2	0.7
31.0-32.9	27.5	0.5
33.0-34.9	25.4	0.5
35.0-36.9	39.8	0.7
37.0-38.9	32.9	0.6
39.0-40.9	16.3	0.2
41.0-42.9	20.6	0.3
43.0-44.9	2.6	†
45.0-46.9	3.5	0.1
47.0 or more	15.5	0.3
Total *	**1,356.4**	**28.1**

† Less than 50,000

* Numbers may not add due to rounding

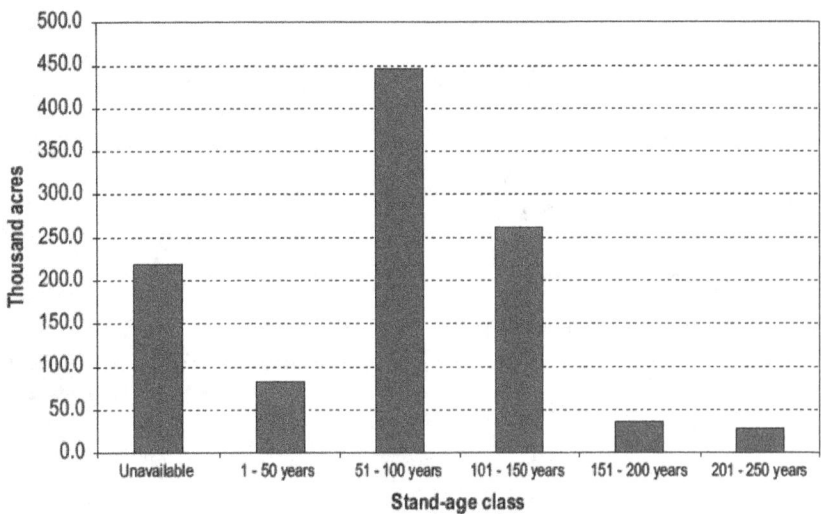

Figure PP 3 – Area of ponderosa pine forest by stand-age class, BLM land.

Thirty percent of the area of ponderosa pine forest is in stands with over 75 square feet per acre of live basal area. Area of ponderosa pine distribution between basal area classes is shown in Figure PP 4. The average is 70 square feet per acre.

The area of ponderosa pine forest by the percent of SDI$_{max}$ is shown in Figure PP 5. About one-third of the stands are considered to be fully occupied (over 35 percent SDI$_{max}$), and half have an SDI that is less than 25 percent SDI$_{max}$. In Oregon, however, stands with at least 35 percent SDI$_{max}$ make up two-thirds of the area.

Snags 5 inches diameter and greater occur on ponderosa pine forest at an average of 9.7 per acre. There are about 10 million snags of this size on ponderosa pine forests. There are an estimated 0.2 large snags per acre (11 inches diameter and greater), and 0.07 very large snags per acre (at least 19 inches diameter). Smaller snags are much more common than larger ones on ponderosa pine forests. Most of the very large snags come from sugar pine and Douglas-fir, with only 14 percent of the very large snags being ponderosa pines. Figure PP 6 shows the distribution of snags in these three size classes.

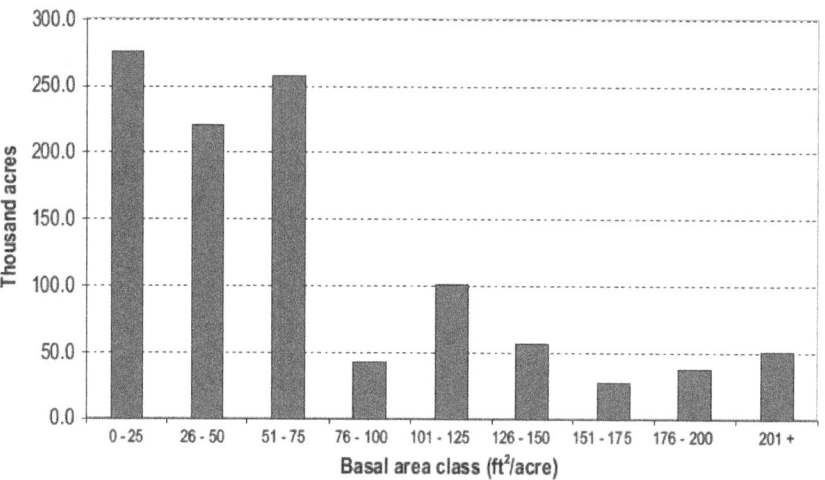

Figure PP 4 – Area of ponderosa pine forest by stand-age class, BLM land.

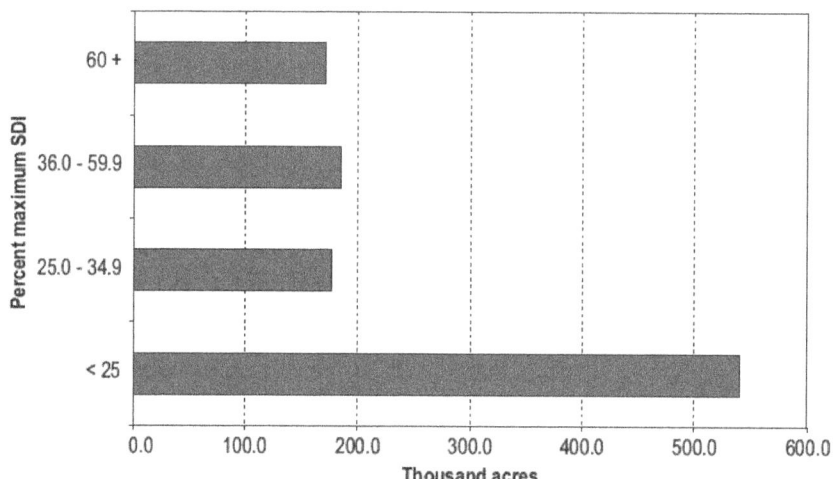

Figure PP 5 – Area of ponderosa pine forest by percent of maximum stand density index (SDI), BLM land.

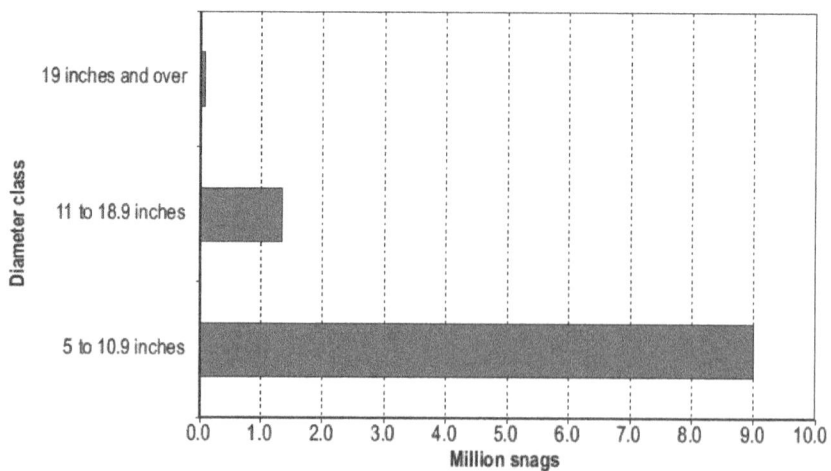

Figure PP 6 – Number of standing dead trees (snags) on ponderosa pine forests by diameter class, BLM land.

Deciduous Oak Woodlands

Deciduous oak woodlands cover about 964 thousand acres on BLM land, about 3 percent of BLM forest land. Deciduous oak woodlands are generally dominated by Gambel oak over most of the forest type's range, but in California the dominant tree is California white oak. Gambel oaks' diameters are measured at the root collar, and California white oaks' are measured at breast height. The woodlands are found at elevations from 1,300 feet in California to nearly 9,000 feet in Colorado, but the lowest-elevation Gambel oak-dominated stands are at about 5,000 feet in Utah. Deciduous oak woodlands occur in six States. (The States and their estimated acreages are listed in Table 2-1.)

Thirty-six percent of live trees 5 inches diameter or more are Gambel oak. The relatively low percentage of the dominant species results from the fact that Gambel oak often occurs in dense thickets of trees less than 5 inches diameter. California white oaks make up about 0.36 percent of all live trees at least 5 inches diameter. Deciduous oak woodland often contains other low-stature species: nearly 48 percent of the trees are a pinyon or juniper species, most often common pinyon. Broadleaf tree species also occur, especially curlleaf mountain-mahogany, with all species (including the two oaks) making up 39 percent of the trees. Tall-stature conifers comprise about 14 percent of the trees, with most being Douglas-firs. Figure DOW 1 shows the area of deciduous oak woodland

by trees-per-acre class, with over 37 percent of the stands having over 1,000 trees per acre. Note that some trees-per-acre classes span intervals greater than 100, due to the absence of stands in some of the 100-tree-per-acre intervals. The average is 1,146 trees per acre, and 21 percent of the area is in stands of less than 100 trees per acre.

Figure DOW 2 shows the distribution of deciduous oak woodland area by stand-size class. Most stands, 92 percent,

are in the sapling/seedling size class, showing how often Gambel oak occurs as smaller-diameter trees. The largest proportion of large-tree stands occurs in California, where the deciduous oak is California white oak.

Deciduous oak woodland stands also tend to be young. The oldest stand age recorded on BLM land was 107 years. Figure DOW 3 shows the area of deciduous oak woodland by stand-age class, using 25-year age classes, rather than 50-year classes as in

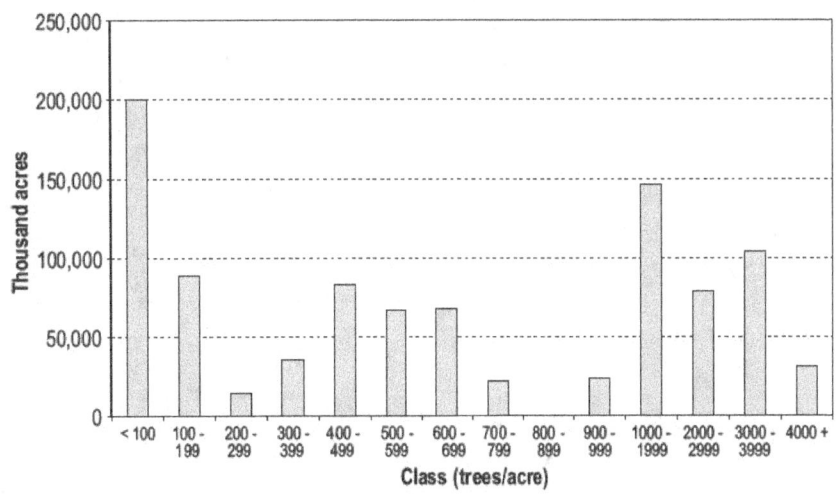

Figure DOW 1 – Area of deciduous oak woodland by trees-per-acre class, BLM land.

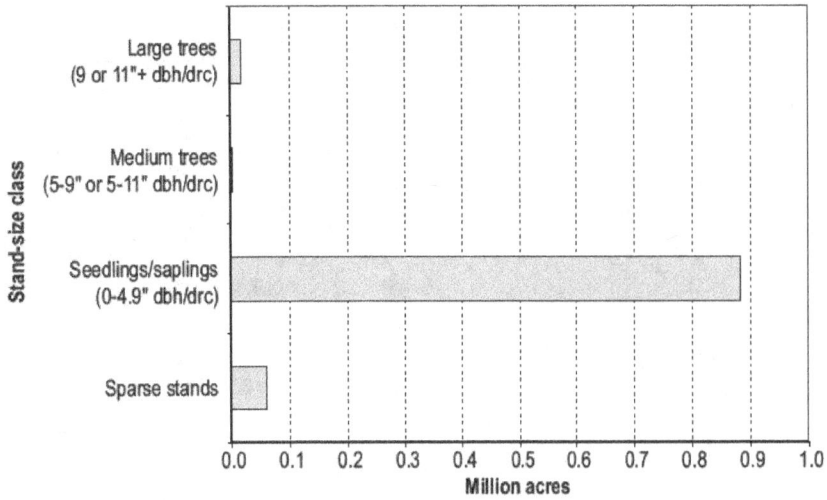

Figure DOW 2 – Area of deciduous oak woodlands by stand-size class, BLM land.

previous forest types. Seventy-four percent of the area is in stands between 1 and 25 years old.

Net live volume and live biomass of deciduous oak woodland by diameter class are shown in Table DOW 1. Only 50 percent of the total biomass comes from the dominant tree, Gambel oak; but, the largest portion of that is in the 1.0 to 2.9 inch diameter class, which is also the diameter class with the highest overall biomass. Ninety-six percent of the biomass in the 1.0 to 2.9 inch size class comes from Gambel oak, again demonstrating the typically small-diameter structure of the species. Gambel oak makes up the majority of the biomass in the three smallest size class, the three classes with the most biomass. Gambel oak makes no contribution to overall biomass in any diameter class 13.0 inches or larger. In these large diameter classes, the largest portion of the biomass comes from ponderosa pine.

Basal area per acre is also low in deciduous oak woodland; only 9 percent of stands have over 75 square feet of live basal area per acre. The distribution of area by basal area class is shown in Figure DOW 4. The average is 39 square feet per acre.

Figure DOW 5 displays the area of deciduous oak woodland by percent of SDI_{max}. Seventeen percent of the area is in stands that are fully occupied, or at least 35 percent SDI_{max}. The largest portion of the area, 70 percent, has SDI values less than 25 percent SDI_{max}. Trees in these stands are considered to be growing without the influence of competition from other trees.

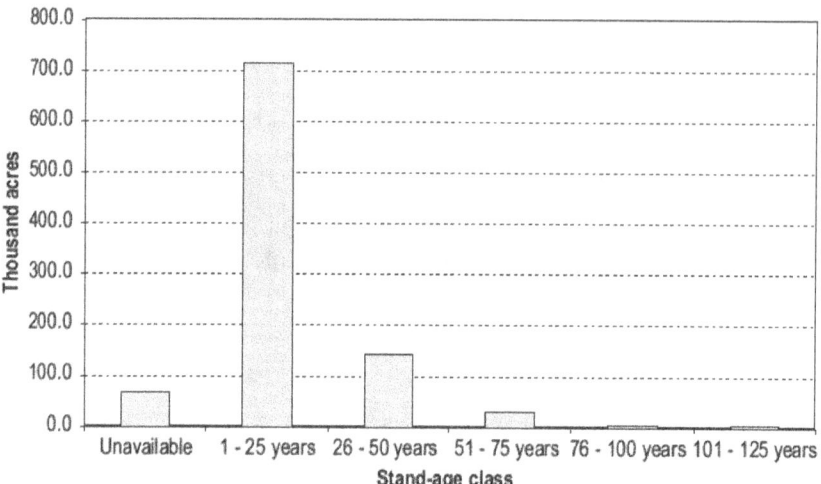

Figure DOW 3 – Area of deciduous oak woodland by stand-age class, BLM land.

Table DOW 1. Net volume and biomass on deciduous oak woodland by diameter class, BLM land.

Diameter class (inches)	Volume (million cubic feet)	Biomass (million tons)
1.0-2.9	--	1.3
3.0-4.9	--	0.9
5.0-6.9	16.6	0.5
7.0-8.9	17.7	0.4
9.0-10.9	9.5	0.2
11.0-12.9	14.9	0.3
13.0-14.9	19.0	0.3
15.0-16.9	8.5	0.1
17.0-18.9	22.7	0.4
19.0-20.9	2.0	†
21.0-22.9	6.9	0.1
23.0-24.9	16.5	0.3
25.0 or more	9.7	0.3
Total *	143.5	5.2

† Less than 50,000

* Numbers may not add due to rounding

Snags 5 inches diameter and larger occur on deciduous oak woodland at the rate of 7.0 per acre, numbering about 6.8 million snags of this size. Snags at least 11 inches diameter average 1.6 per acre, and snags 19 inches diameter average 0.2 per acre. Very large snags on deciduous oak woodland were all Douglas-firs and ponderosa pines. The distribution of snags by these three size classes is shown in Figure DOW 6.

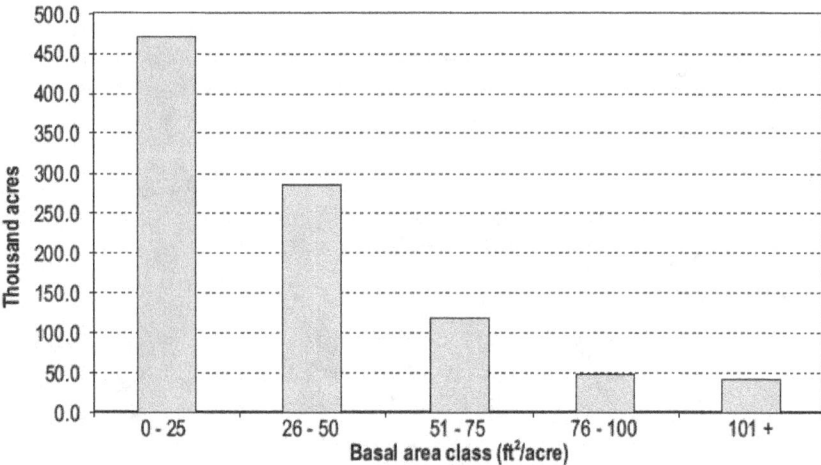

Figure DOW 4 – Area of deciduous oak woodland by live-tree basal area class, BLM land.

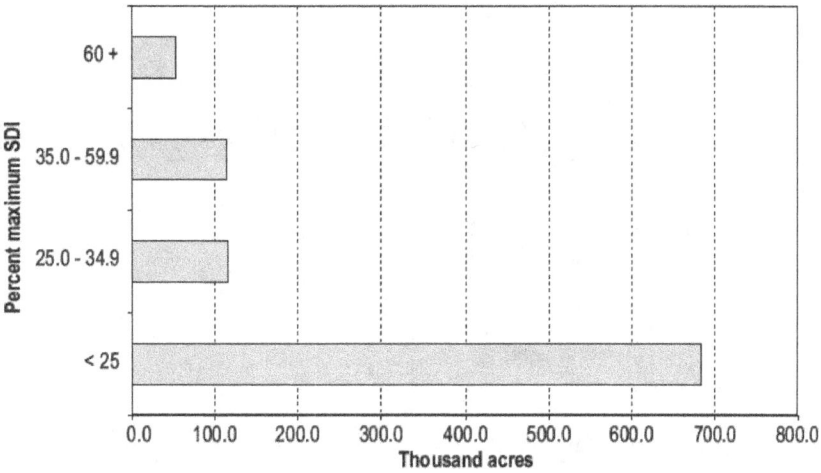

Figure DOW 5 – Area of deciduous oak woodland by percent of maximum stand density (SDI), BLM land.

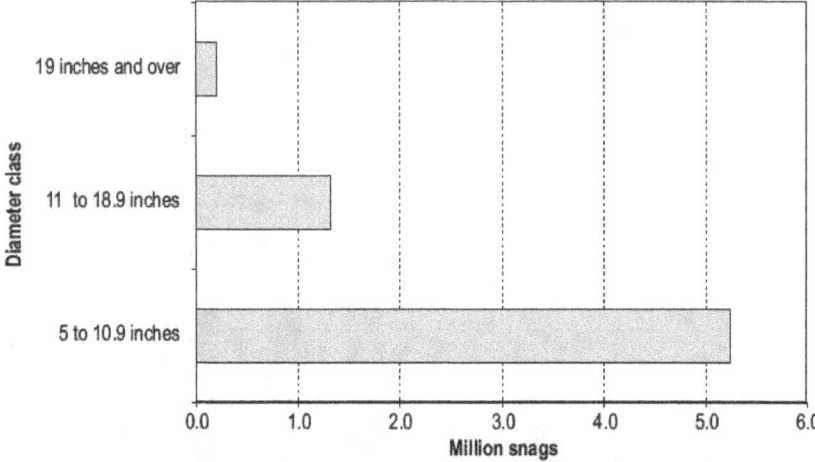

Figure DOW 6 – Number of standing dead trees (snags) on deciduous oak woodlands by diameter class, BLM land.

Cercocarpus Woodlands

About 642 thousand acres of BLM forest land, about 2 percent, is *Cercocarpus* woodland, which are dominated by curlleaf mountain-mahogany. The forest type name comes from the Latin designation for this species: *Cercocarpus ledifolius*. Eighty-eight percent of the live trees 5 inches diameter and larger are curlleaf mountain-mahogany. Diameters for curlleaf mountain-mahogany are taken at the root collar. In this type, pinyons and junipers make up 9 percent of the trees of this size, with singleleaf pinyon being the most common. Three percent of all trees are tall conifers, and less than 1 percent are other broadleaf species.

Cercocarpus woodland stands average 430 trees per acre, with 24 percent of the stands having less than 100 trees per acre and 25 percent with over 400 trees per acre. Figure CW 1 displays the area of *Cercocarpus* woodland by trees per acre. It occurs in eight States at elevations ranging from 3,100 feet in California to over 9,000 feet in Nevada. (The States and their estimated acreages are listed in Table 2-1.)

The majority, 60 percent, of *Cercocarpus* woodland area is in the large-tree stand-size class. Stands in the medium-tree and the seedling/sapling stand-size classes each make up 16 percent of the area, while those in the sparse stand size comprise 8 percent. Figure CW 2 displays the area by stand-size class.

Figure CW 3 shows how stand-age classes are distributed over *Cercocarpus* woodland area. Since the oldest stand age was

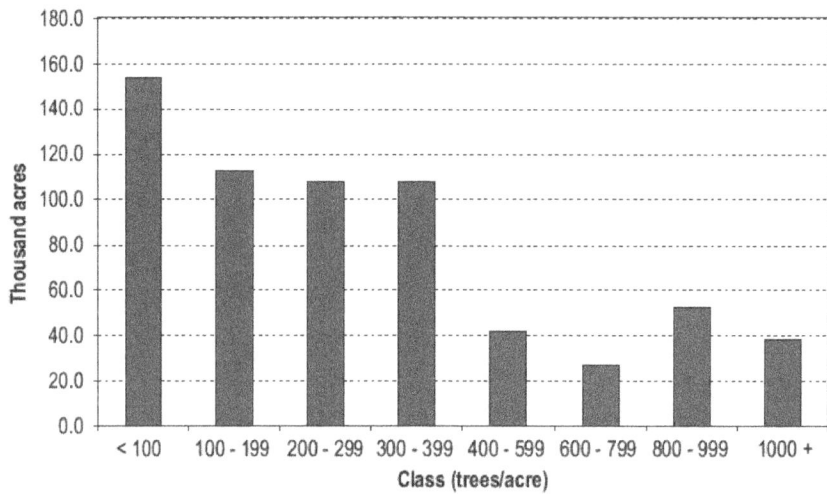

Figure CW 1 – Area of *Cercocarpus* woodland by trees-per-acre class, BLM land.

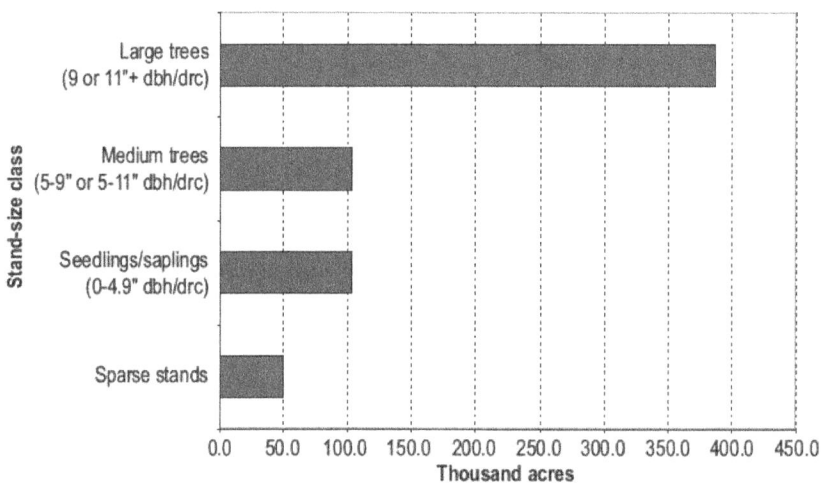

Figure CW 2 – Area of *Cercocarpus* woodland by stand-size class, BLM land.

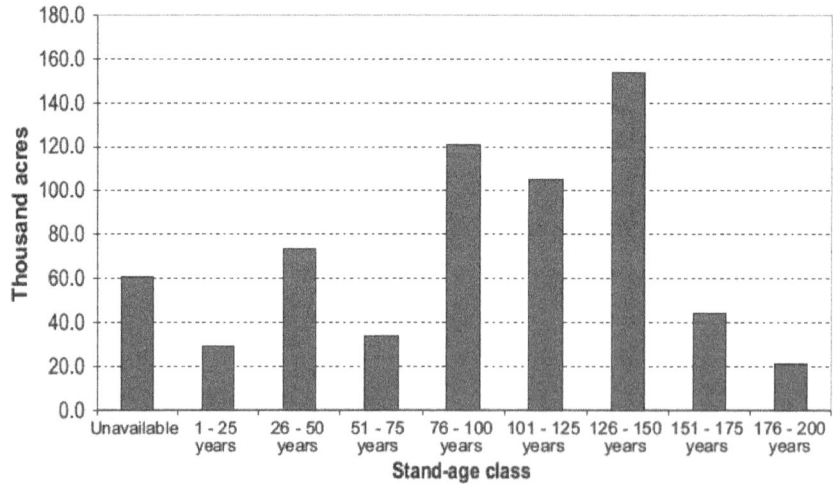

Figure CW 3 – Area of *Cercocarpus* woodland by stand-age class, BLM land.

200 years, the distribution is displayed by 25-year classes. The most common class is 126 to 150 years, with 24 percent of the area.

Net live volume and live biomass for live trees on *Cercocarpus* woodland are shown by diameter class in table CW 1. Eighty-two percent of the volume comes from curlleaf mountain-mahogany. Other species making significant biomass contributions are singleleaf pinyon at 6 percent, and Douglas-fir and white fir with 3 percent each.

The average *Cercocarpus* woodland stand has 75 square feet of live basal area per acre. Forty-one percent of the area has over 75 square feet of live basal area per acre. The distribution of the area of *Cercocarpus* woodlands by basal area classes is shown in Figure CW 4.

Forty-one percent of the area of *Cercocarpus* woodland on BLM land has an SDI of at least 35 percent of the SDI_{max}, indicating full stand occupancy. Forty-two percent are not dense enough for the competition between trees to have begun (less than 25 percent SDI_{max}), and 17 percent (between 25 and 34.9 percent SDI_{max}) are showing signs of competition, but are not yet fully occupied. Figure CW 5 displays the distribution of *cercocarpus* woodland area by the percent SDI_{max}. The stands with full occupancy are divided between those that have begun self-thinning (over 60 percent SDI_{max}, 16 percent of all stands) and those not yet dense enough to begin self thinning (35 to 60 percent SDI_{max}, 26 percent of all stands).

Table CW 1. Net live volume and live biomass on *Cercocarpus* woodland by diameter class, BLM land.

Diameter class (inches)	Volume (million cubic feet)	Biomass (million tons)
1.0-2.9	–	0.2
3.0-4.9	–	0.6
5.0-6.9	19.9	0.8
7.0-8.9	24.2	0.9
9.0-10.9	29.7	1.1
11.0-12.9	35.6	1.2
13.0-14.9	20.1	0.7
15.0-16.9	21.7	0.7
17.0-18.9	14.6	0.6
19.0-20.9	4.5	0.1
21.0-22.9	4.1	0.1
23.0-24.9	13.0	0.4
25.0-26.9	0.5	†
27.0-28.9	2.2	0.1
29.0 or more	0.2	†
Total *	190.3	7.5

† Less than 50,000

* Numbers may not add due to rounding

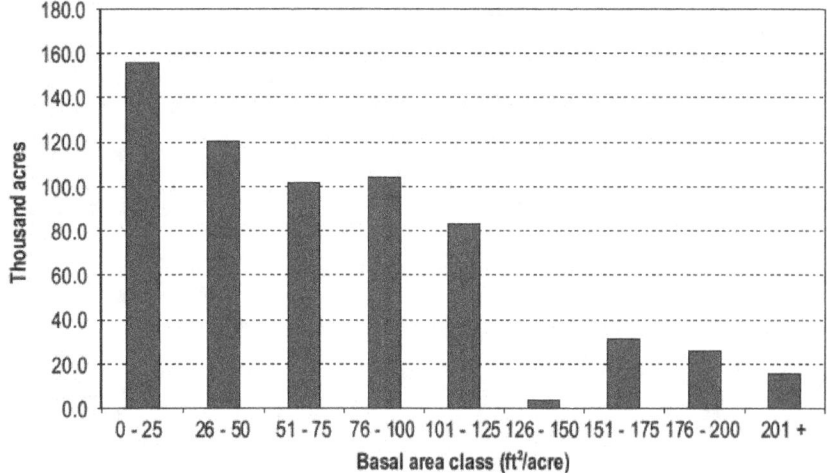

Figure CW 4 – Area of *Cercocarpus* woodland by live-tree basal area class, BLM land.

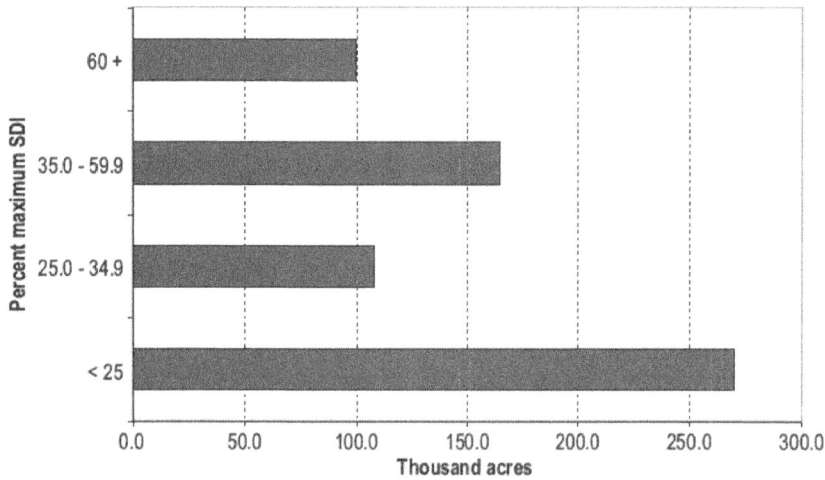

Figure CW 5 – Area of *Cercocarpus* woodland by percent of maximum stand density index (SDI), BLM land.

About 13 million snags are found on *Cercocarpus* woodlands, for a density of 20 snags per acre. Larger snags are found at densities of 4.2 snags per acre for all snags 11 inches diameter and over, and 0.7 for snags at least 19 inches diameter. These very large snags (19 inches diameter or more) are mostly from limber pine and singleaf pinyon, with some western junipers and curlleaf mountain mahoganies. The distribution of snags in the three sizes is shown in Figure CW 6.

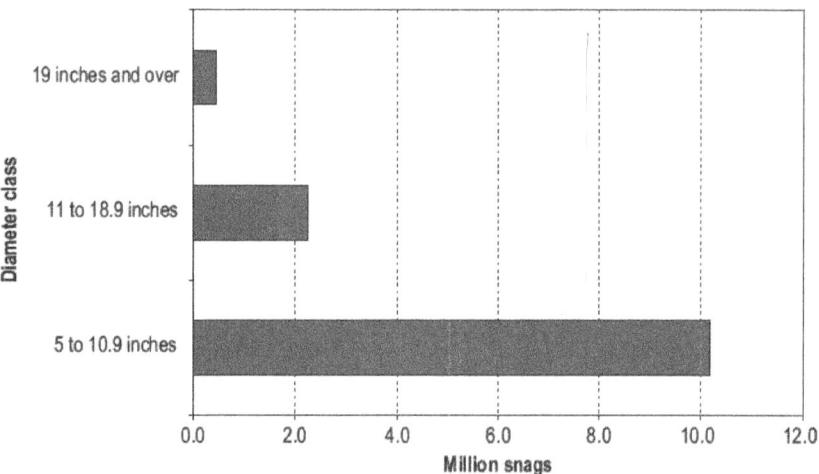

Figure CW 6 – Number of standing dead trees (snags) on *Cercocarpus* woodlands by diameter class, BLM land.

Aspen Forests

Aspen forests cover 368 thousand acres, or just over 1 percent, of BLM forest land. Nearly 80 percent of live trees 5 inches diameter or larger are quaking aspens. Aside from a few Gambel oak (less than 1 percent of the trees), all the other live trees at least 5 inches diameter sampled in aspen forests were tall-stature conifers. The most common among these are Douglas-fir and subalpine fir.

The average aspen stand on BLM land has 422 trees per acre, with 22 percent having less than 100 trees per acre and 17 percent having 500 or more trees per acre. Figure AS 1 displays the distribution of aspen forest acreage by trees-per-acre class. Aspen forests on BLM lands are found in six States ranging in elevation from 5,700 feet in Oregon to over 10,200 feet in Colorado. (The States and their estimated acreages by forest type, including aspen forests, are listed in Table 2-1.)

The area of aspen forest by stand-size class is shown in Figure AS 2, indicating that 58 percent of the area is in the medium-tree size class. This reflects that aspen trees are, on average, smaller than in other tall-stature types, and also that the division between medium and large trees in quaking aspen, classified as a hardwood, is at 11 inches diameter, rather than 9 inches as in softwoods (conifers). Twenty-two percent of the stands are in the seedlings/saplings size class, and 17 percent are in the large-tree class. Less than 4 percent of the acreage is classified in the sparse stands class. This may be because aspen is often an early colonizer of disturbed stands that might have been another forest type before the disturbance. If aspen regeneration is not evident at the time of plot measurement, the field crews would likely assign the "nonstocked," or sparse stand size class to the previous forest type. If aspen regeneration was well underway, the size class would be seedling/sapling.

Aspen is a relatively short-lived species and the data collected from BLM land reflects this characteristic, with the oldest stand age recorded for aspen forests on BLM land at 200 years. Half of the stands are between 75 and 100 years old. Aspen age class distribution is shown on Figure AS 3.

Net live volume and live biomass are listed by diameter classes in Table AS 1. Sixty-six percent of the volume is in quaking aspens, and 34 percent is in tall-stature conifers (Gambel oak provides 0.1 percent of the volume, all in

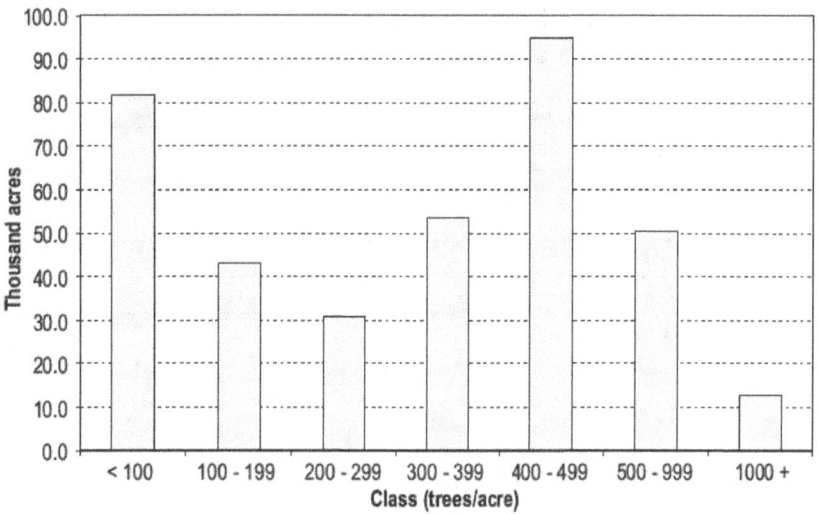

Figure AS 1 – Area of aspen forest by trees-per-acre class, BLM land.

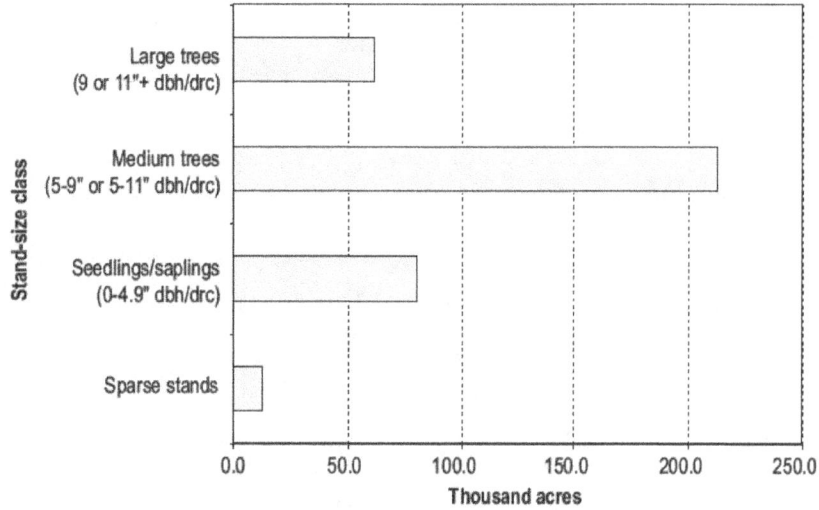

Figure AS 2 – Area of aspen forest by stand-size class, BLM land.

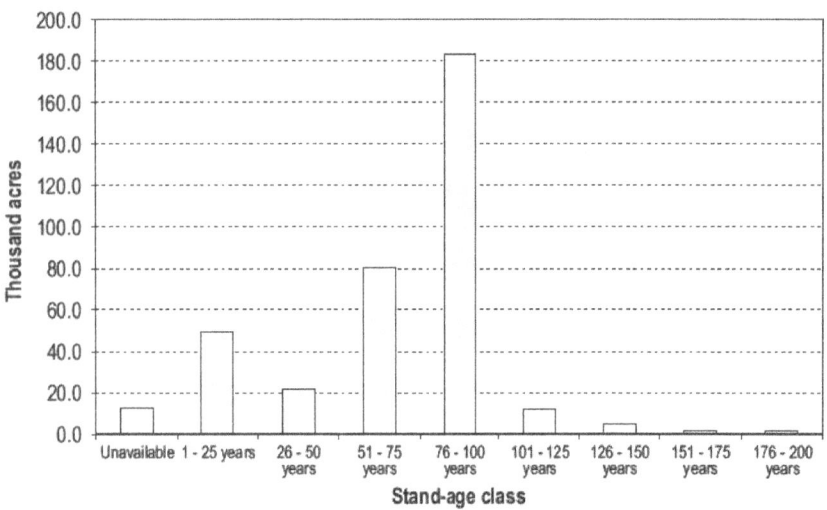

Figure AS 3 – Area of aspen forest by stand-age class, BLM land.

Table AS 1. Net live volume and live biomass on aspen forests by diameter class, BLM land.

Diameter class (inches)	Volume (million cubic feet)	Biomass (million tons)
1.0-2.9	–	0.2
3.0-4.9	–	0.2
5.0-6.9	36.5	0.7
7.0-8.9	86.6	1.5
9.0-10.9	112.5	1.9
11.0-12.9	84.4	1.5
13.0-14.9	26.1	0.4
15.0-16.9	14.3	0.3
17.0-18.9	29.8	0.5
19.0-20.9	24.3	0.5
21.0-22.9	21.8	0.4
Total *	436.4	8.0

* Numbers may not add due to rounding

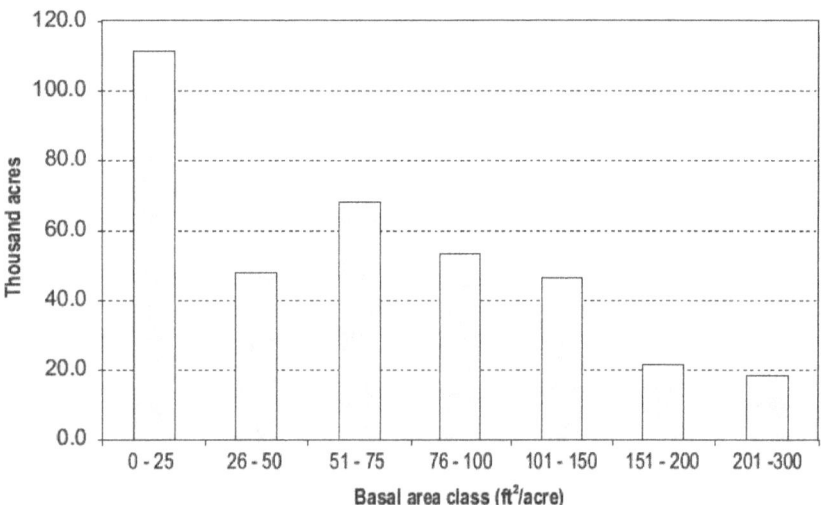

Figure AS 4 – Area of aspen forest by live-tree basal area class, BLM land.

the 5.0 to 6.9 inch diameter class). In smaller diameters, up to 14.9 inches, the majority of the net live volume is in quaking aspens. Most of the volume in larger diameter classes is in conifers, and all of the volume in the 21.0 to 22.9 inch diameter class is in Douglas-firs and subalpine firs.

The area of aspen forests by live tree basal area per acre is shown in Figure AS 4, with the largest proportion of the area, 30 percent, having 25 square feet per acre or less. Thirty-eight percent of the stands have over 75 square feet per acre in basal area, with the average stand at 72 square feet per acre of live basal area.

Thirty percent of the acreage in aspen forests is considered to be fully occupied, as shown by an SDI of 35 percent or more of the SDI_{max} for aspen forests. Over 50 percent of the area is in stands considered to be sparse enough that competition between individual trees is insignificant (less than 25 percent SDI_{max}). The area of aspen forests by percent of SDI_{max} is shown in Figure AS 5. Twenty percent of the stands are between 25 and 34.9 percent SDI_{max}. The fully-occupied stands include 17 percent that are not at the onset of self-thinning and 13 percent that are likely to be undergoing self-thinning through mortality.

Over 11 million snags, at least 5 inches diameter, are estimated to occur on BLM aspen forests. The distribution of snags by diameter class is shown in Figure AS 6. The average density is 30 snags per acre, with larger snag densities

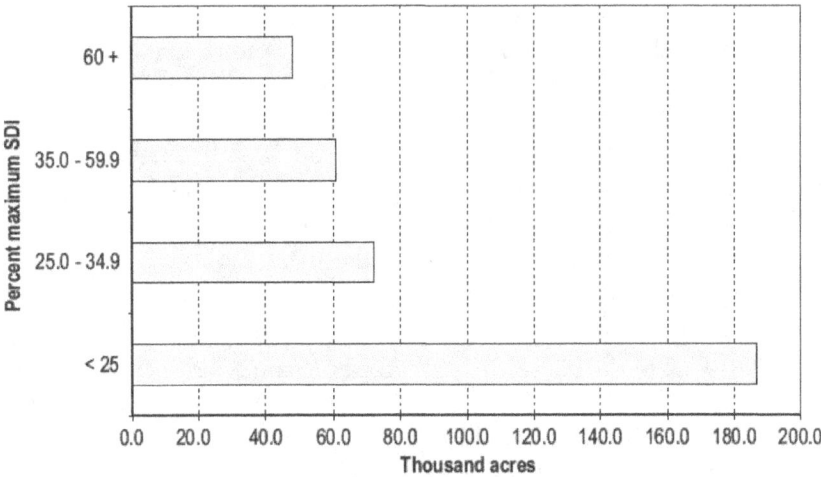

Figure AS 5 – Area of aspen forest by stand-age class, BLM land.

at 2.4 snags per acre at least 11 inches diameter, and 0.15 snags per acre 19 inches diameter or larger. Two-thirds of all snags are from quaking aspen. However, these snag data present an illustration of the effect of single plots on smaller data sets, as well as an example of aspen regeneration. The estimates for 11 percent of the snags (including all of the snags over 19 inches diameter) were derived from conifers killed by fire on one plot. At the time of plot measurement, the stand was regenerating in aspen and was in the seedlings/saplings stand-size class.

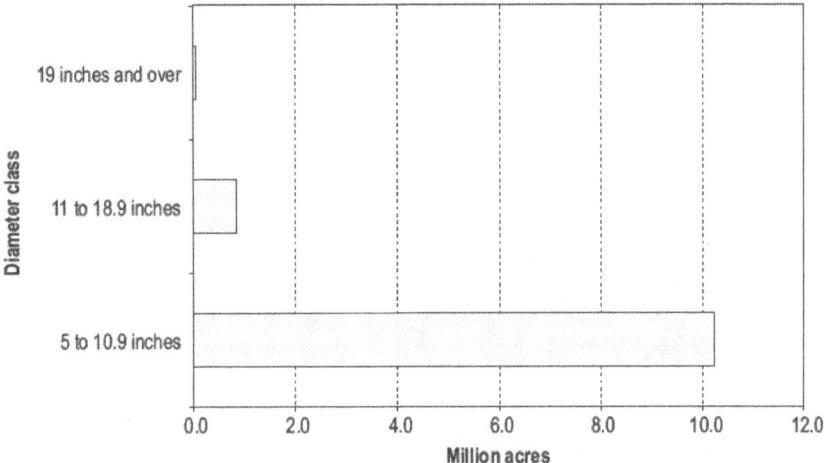

Figure AS 6 – Number of standing dead trees (snags) on aspen forests by diameter class, BLM land.

Lodgepole Pine Forests

Just over 1 percent of BLM forest land (359 thousand acres) consists of lodgepole pine forests. Eighty-eight percent of the live trees 5 inches diameter and greater in this forest type are lodgepole pine trees. All of the trees sampled are tall stature species, and with the exception of quaking aspen (which makes up 1 percent of the trees), all are conifers. The most common trees, other than lodgepole pines, are Douglas-firs and subalpine firs, comprising 6 percent and 3 percent, respectively, of all the live trees at least 5 inches diameter.

Lodgepole pine forests on BLM land are found in four States, and at elevations as low as 100 feet in Oregon and as high as 10,100 feet in Colorado. (Table 2-1 lists the estimates of the area of lodgepole pine forest in acres for each of the States.)

Lodgepole pine stands average 527 live trees per acre. Stands with less than 100 trees per acre make up 15 percent of the area, and those with 1,000 or more trees per acre make up 7 percent. Figure LP 1 shows how lodgepole pine forest area is distributed by trees-per-acre class. The groupings for 500 trees per acre and more are in 250 tree-per-acre increments, rather than 100 tree-per-acre increments, due to missing values in some 100 tree-per-acre classes.

Forty-two percent of the area of lodgepole pine forests is in the medium-tree stand-size class and 34 percent is in the large-tree stand-size class. The area of lodgepole pine forest in each of the stand-size classes is shown in Figure LP 2. Twenty-

two percent is in the seedlings/saplings size class, and 2 percent is classified as sparse stands.

Figure LP 3 displays the area of lodgepole pine by stand age in 25-year classes. The oldest stand age for lodgepole pine forest was 166 years, and 35 percent of the area is in stands that are between 101 and 125 years old.

Table LP 1 lists the net live volume and live biomass by diameter class for lodgepole pine forests. Volume and biomass are the highest in the 9.0 to 10.9 inch class. Eighty-seven percent of the net live

volume is in lodgepole pine trees. All of the volume in diameter classes 11 inches and larger comes from lodgepole pine, Douglas-fir, subalpine fir, and limber pine, with only Douglas-fir and limber pine volume represented in the 19.0 to 20.9 inch class.

The distribution of the area of lodgepole pine forests by live tree basal area class is shown in Figure LP 4. The average lodgepole pine stand has 104 square feet of basal area per acre, with 72 percent of stands having over 75 square feet per acre of live tree basal area. These numbers are second only

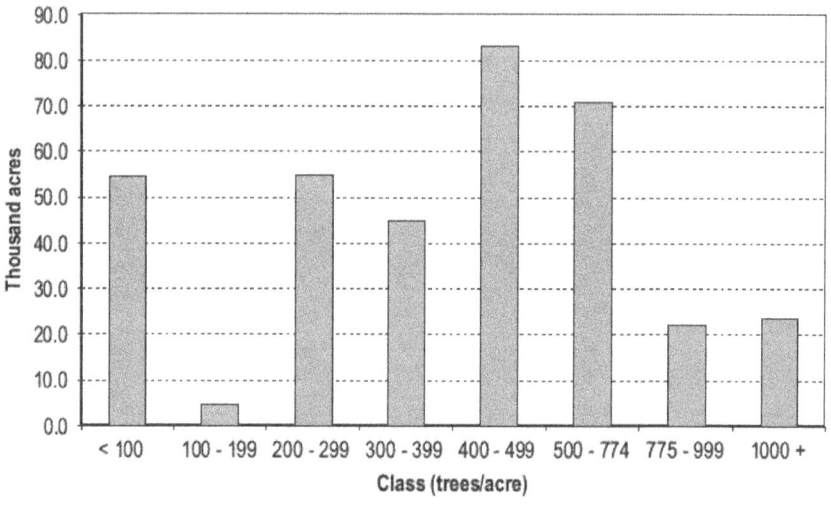

Figure LP 1 – Area of lodgepole pine forest by trees-per-acre class, BLM land.

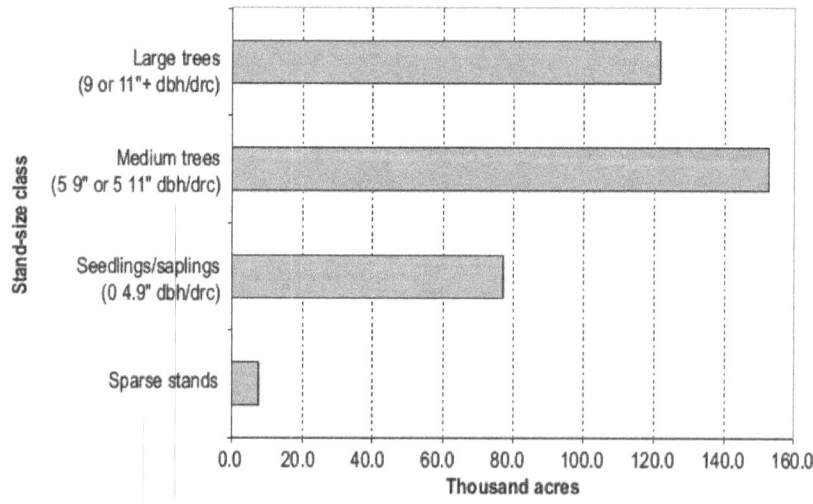

Figure LP 2 – Area of lodgepole pine forest by stand-size class, BLM land.

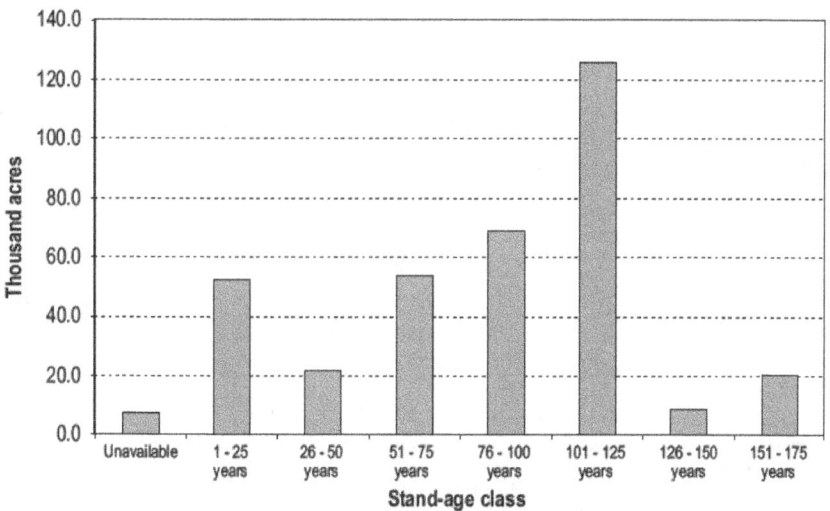

Figure LP 3 – Area of lodgepole pine forest by stand-age class, BLM land.

Table LP 1. Net live volume and live biomass on lodgepole pine forests by diameter class, BLM land.

Diameter class (inches)	Volume (million cubic feet)	Biomass (million tons)
1.0-2.9	–	0.3
3.0-4.9	–	0.6
5.0-6.9	125.6	2.6
7.0-8.9	173.9	2.9
9.0-10.9	222.0	3.6
11.0-12.9	108.3	1.8
13.0-14.9	51.6	0.9
15.0-16.9	22.7	0.4
17.0-18.9	13.5	0.2
19.0-20.9	5.2	0.1
Total *	722.8	13.2

* Numbers may not add due to rounding

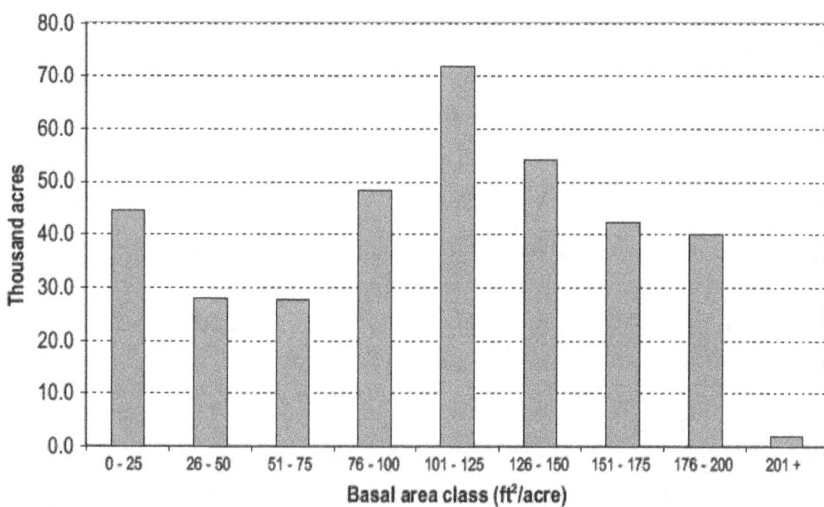

Figure LP 4 – Area of lodgepole pine forest by live-tree basal area class, BLM land.

to coastal Douglas-fir, and since the tree diameters for lodgepole pine are much lower than those for Douglas-fir, they indicate how dense these relatively small-diameter stands can sometimes be.

Sixty-nine percent of the lodgepole pine area is in stands that are considered fully occupied, as indicated by an SDI of 35 percent or more of the SDI_{max}. Fifty-five percent of all stands are fully occupied, but before the onset of mortality-related self thinning (35 to 60 percent SDI_{max}). These results also indicate dense stands of medium trees and large trees less than 19 inches diameter, especially considering an average of over 500 trees per acre. Figure LP 5 shows the area of lodgepole pine forests by percent SDI_{max}. Twenty-eight percent of the area is in stands with less than 25 percent SDI_{max} (less dense stands where competition between trees is not a factor), and just less than 4 percent of the area is between 25 and 34.9 percent SDI_{max}.

About 11.8 million snags are estimated to occur in lodgepole pine forests on BLM-managed lands. This averages out to 33 snags per acre, which is the most for any forest type discussed in this report. This is 11.8 percent of all trees at least 5 inches diameter, which is higher than any other major BLM forest type. The average for lodgepole pine forests over all ownerships is 46 snags per acre. Larger dead trees (11 inches diameter or larger) average 1.5 snags per acre, and very large snags (at least 19 inches diameter) occur at 0.2 per acre. Figure LP 6 displays the number of snags in each of these diameter classes. Both the 11 to18.9 inch class and the 19

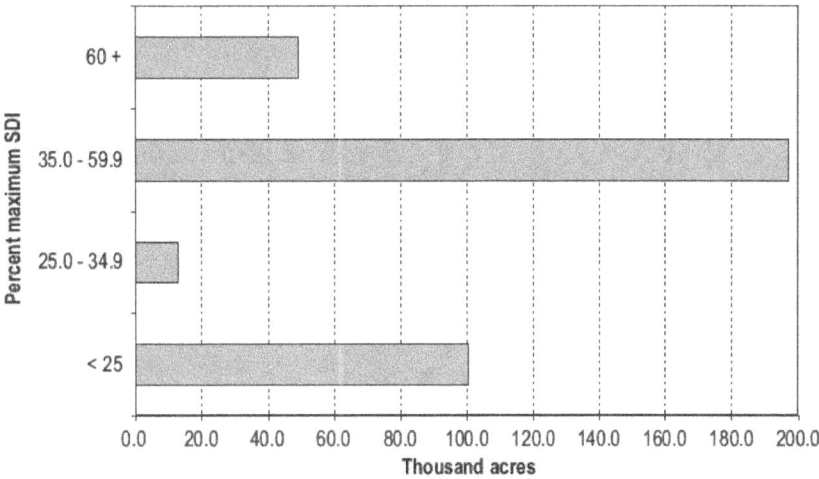

Figure LP 5 – Area of lodgepole pine forest by percent of maximum stand density index (SDI), BLM land.

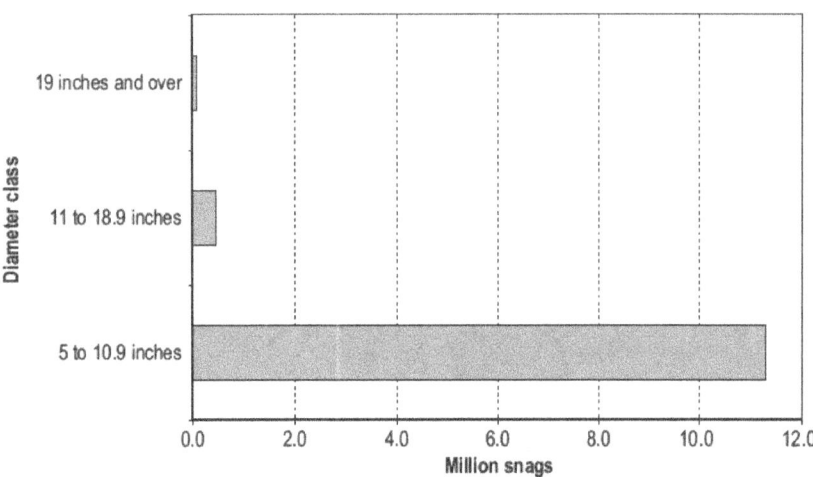

Figure LP 6 – Number of standing dead trees (snags) on lodgepole pine forests by diameter class, BLM land.

inches and over class consist of 60 percent Douglas-fir snags and 40 percent lodgepole pine snags.

A major concern for managers of lodgepole pine forests is the risk of widespread mortality due to outbreaks of mountain pine beetle. There are several published methods for assessing mountain pine beetle risk in lodgepole pine forest, and two are used by the USDA Forest Service's Forest Health Technology Enterprise Team (FHTET) as the basis for extensions to the Forest Vegetation Simulator (FVS) modeling tool (USDA 2005b) for evaluating mountain pine beetle risk. The

simpler of the two is based on Amman et al. (1977). This method evaluates risk based on three factors: elevation/latitude, stand age, and average diameter, and assigns three levels of risk factor to each (1 for low risk, 2 for medium risk, and 3 for high risk). The elevation risk factor is low for high elevations, and high for low elevations. Exactly where the threshold breaks are for the elevation risk factor is best determined by local conditions and knowledge, but a "first approximation" is based on a hypothesized linear relationship between elevation, latitude, and risk.

Using the first approximation equations, an elevation/latitude risk factor of 3 was assigned to 30 percent of the area of BLM lodgepole pine forests. The stand age risk factor breaks are at 60 and 80 years (lower risk for younger stands). Sixty-two percent of stands have an age risk factor of 3. Diameter risk is based on the average diameter of all trees greater than 5 inches DBH in the stand, and the risk factor breaks are at 7 and 8 inches average DBH (lower risk for smaller stands). For diameter risk factors, 58 percent of the area was assigned a factor of 3. To be judged as having an overall high risk rating for mountain pine beetle outbreak, all three risk factors must have a risk factor of 3. Ten percent of the area of BLM lodgepole pine forests is judged to be at high risk of mountain pine beetle outbreak. High-risk stands occurred in Montana and Colorado. Forty-two percent of the area has moderate risk, and 49 percent has low risk. The maximum combined risk factor value in the moderate-risk category, in which two of the factors are rated 3 and one is rated 2, was also evaluated. Thirty percent of the area fell into this category, with all three possible combinations present. The most common of these combinations, with 25 percent of the total area, has factors of 3 for age and diameter risk and 2 for elevation risk. Since the elevation risk was based on first approximation, and is better evaluated locally, stands with risk factors of 3 for both age and diameter should be regarded as at substantial risk of mountain pine beetle outbreak. Altogether, 37 percent of all BLM lodgepole pine stands are in this category, occurring in Montana, Colorado, and Wyoming.

Chapter 3—BLM Forest Land by State

Background

The different methodologies used by FIA (e.g., periodic and annual inventories), as mentioned previously in the Introduction, have influenced this report. Wyoming and New Mexico have not yet been added to the annual inventory, and the other States are at various stages in the annual cycle. One result is that the plot density, measured by the forest land acreage represented by each sample plot, varies by State. Each State discussion provides plot density for that State, which affects sampling error, both for estimates based on plot measurements, like forest land acreages, and for those based on tree measurements, like wood volume. Therefore, the forest land acreage and the cubic foot net volume are provided for each State along with the appropriate percent standard error.

Additionally, while the IW-FIA has developed methods for measuring and reporting growth and mortality for individual trees during the first annual inventory cycle, other FIA units have not. As a result, growth figures (in terms of **gross annual growth, net annual growth,** and **mortality**) are provided in all States except for California, Oregon, Washington, and North and South Dakota.

Arizona

The BLM manages over 12 million acres of land in Arizona of which 15 percent (1.9 million acres) is forested. Fifty-four percent of this area is pinyon/juniper woodlands, and 27 percent is juniper woodlands. The most abundant forest type not described in Chapter 2 of this report is mesquite woodland, which comprises about 16 percent of the BLM forest land in Arizona. The only tall-stature forest type encountered on BLM land was ponderosa pine forest. Figure AZ 1 shows the area of forest land by forest type and stand-size class.

The data for Arizona were collected on the annual grid from 2001 to 2005 by IW-FIA crews. These 5 years account for 50 percent of the 10-year annual cycle. Forests and woodlands were sampled on 163 condition proportions, representing an average of about 11,600 acres per plot condition. Table AZ 1 shows the estimates and standard errors for representative variables on Arizona BLM forest land.

BLM forest land in Arizona contains an estimated 640 million cubic feet in live wood net volume. Gross annual growth is 5.9 million cubic feet and annual mortality is 1.9 million cubic feet, yielding a net annual growth of 4 million cubic feet. Figure AZ 2 displays gross growth and mortality by species. "Other softwoods" with measured mortality were California and redberry junipers; the "other hardwood" with measured mortality was Emory oak. The highest mortality occurred in common pinyons, where mortality was 91 percent of growth. Ninety-seven percent of the common pinyon mortality was caused by insects, which were the overall leading cause of mortality, contributing to 48 percent, including 17 percent of singleleaf pinyon mortality. Shaw et al. (2005) provides a more detailed analysis of recent pinyon mortality. Mortality in Utah junipers was caused by weather, vegetation, or unknown causes in roughly equal proportions.

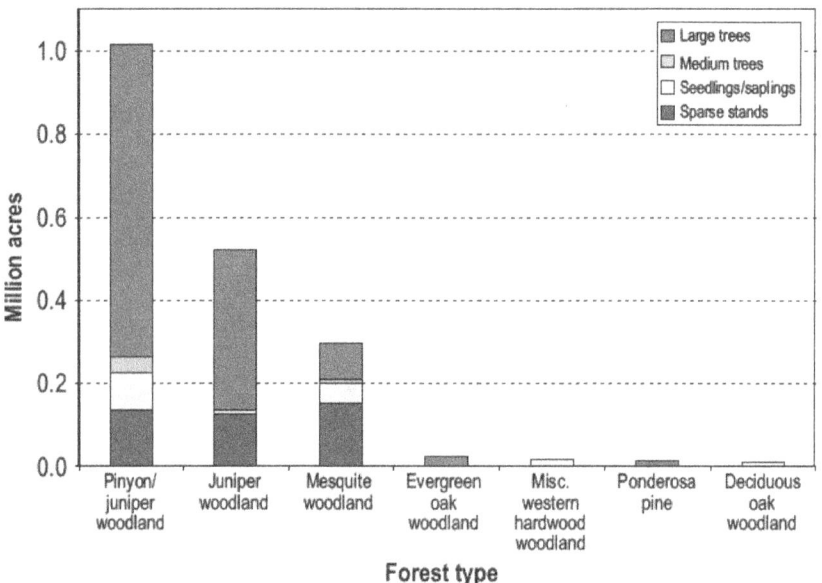

Figure AZ 1 – Area of forest land by forest type and stand-size class, Arizona BLM land.

Table AZ 1. Percent standard error for area of forest land and net volume for all live trees on BLM land in Arizona.

Variable	Units	Estimate	Percent standard error
Forest land	Acres	1,893,439	± 6.98
Net live tree volume	Cubic feet	640,277,334	± 9.77

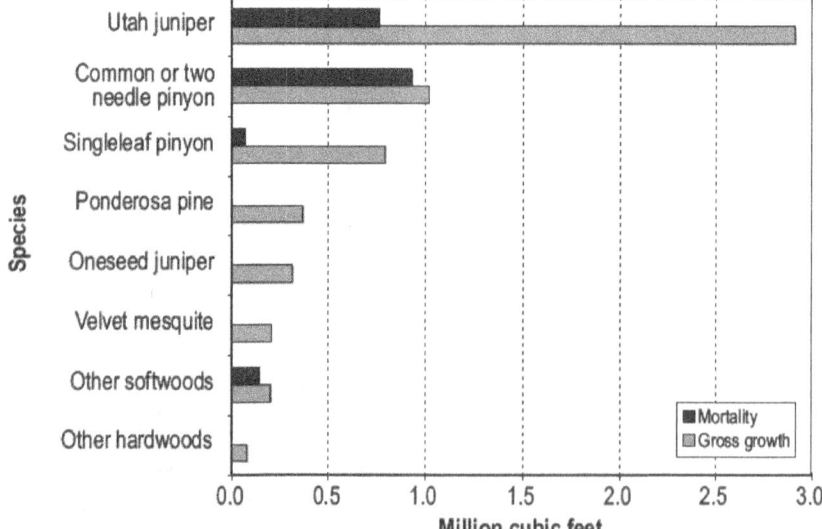

Figure AZ 2 – Gross annual growth of all live trees 5.0 inches diameter and greater compared to mortality by species, Arizona BLM land.

California

The BLM manages over 15 million acres in California and about 10 percent (1.4 million acres) of it is forested. Eighteen different forest and woodland types have been encountered on BLM lands in California. The most common are pinyon/juniper woodlands at 21 percent of the area and western juniper at 19 percent of the area. California has the largest proportion of its area, 44 percent, in forest types not described in Chapter 2 of this report. The most common of these is canyon live oak/interior live oak with 16 percent of the area and also blue oak, California mixed conifer, tanoak, and Oregon white oak. Figure CA 1 shows the area of BLM forest land in California by forest type and stand-size class. "Other types" in the figure include mesquite woodlands, California black oak, gray pine, miscellaneous western softwoods, Douglas-fir forests, miscellaneous western hardwood woodlands, cottonwood/willow, deciduous oak woodlands, and Oregon ash forests.

California data used in this report came from 4 years of annual inventory (2001–2004) collected by PNW-FIA. This represents 40 percent of the annual grid for the State. Measurements of BLM forestland were taken on 113 condition proportions, so each plot condition represents about 12,800 acres. Estimates and standard errors for representative variables are listed in table CA 1.

There are 1.3 billion net cubic feet of wood volume in all the live trees at least 5 inches diameter on BLM land in California. Most of the volume is in forest types not described in Chapter 2 of this report: canyon live oak/interior live oak, California mixed conifer, and tanoak contain 67 percent of the net live volume. A major proportion of the volume in each of these types is in Douglas-fir trees, and Douglas-firs contribute 51 percent of the volume in the three types combined. On a tree species basis, 41 percent of all volume is in Douglas-fir trees. No data are currently available for growth and mortality in California.

Table CA 1. Percent standard error for area of forest land and net volume for all live trees on BLM land in California.

Variable	Units	Estimate	Percent standard error
Forest land	Acres	1,449,197	± 8.98
Net live tree volume	Cubic feet	1,289,503,064	± 20.17

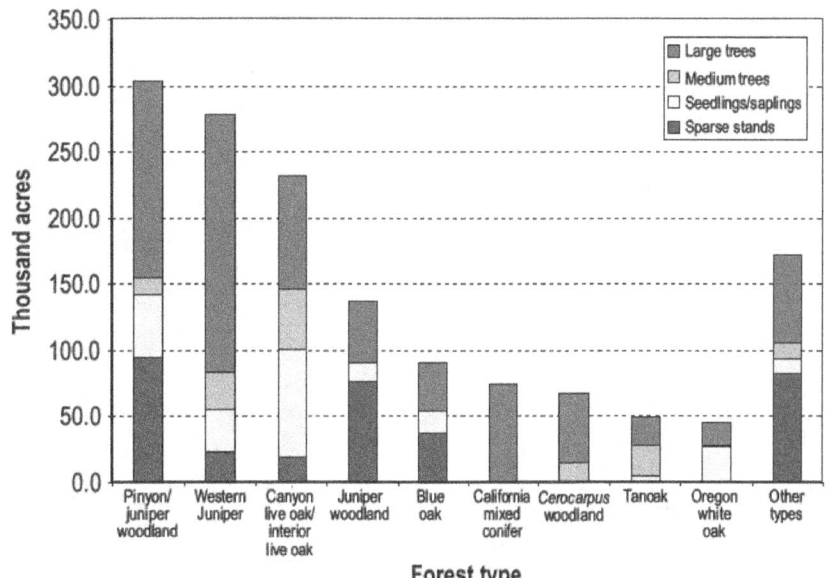

Figure CA 1 – Area of forestland by forest type and stand-size class, California BLM land.

Colorado

The BLM manages over 8 million acres in Colorado and about 61 percent (5 million acres) is estimated to be forested. This is the highest percentage of BLM lands that are forested in any State. Fifty-six percent of Colorado's BLM forests are pinyon/juniper woodlands and 13 percent are juniper woodlands. Deciduous oak woodlands follow at 11 percent. The most common tall-stature forest type is Douglas-fir with nearly 5 percent of the forest land. The most common forest type not discussed in Chapter 2 of this report is Engelmann spruce

forest. Figure CO 1 shows the area of forest land by forest type and stand-size class. "Other types" in this figure include subalpine fir forests, *Cercocarpus* woodlands, and cottonwood forests.

The data for Colorado are from the annual inventory, collected by IW-FIA between 2002–2005. These 4 years of data collection represent 40 percent of the annual grid with a 10-year annual cycle. The data were collected on 360 forested conditions, each plot condition representing about 14,100 acres. Estimates and standard errors for representative variables are presented in table CO 1.

Table CO 1. Percent standard error for area of forest land and net volume for all live trees on BLM land in Colorado.

Variable	Units	Estimate	Percent standard error
Forest land	Acres	5,076,439	± 4.46
Net live tree volume	Cubic feet	4,219,948,006	± 7.56

Net live volume for all BLM woodlands and forests in Colorado is 4.2 billion cubic feet. Gross annual growth is estimated at 48 million cubic feet and the annual mortality estimate is 19 million

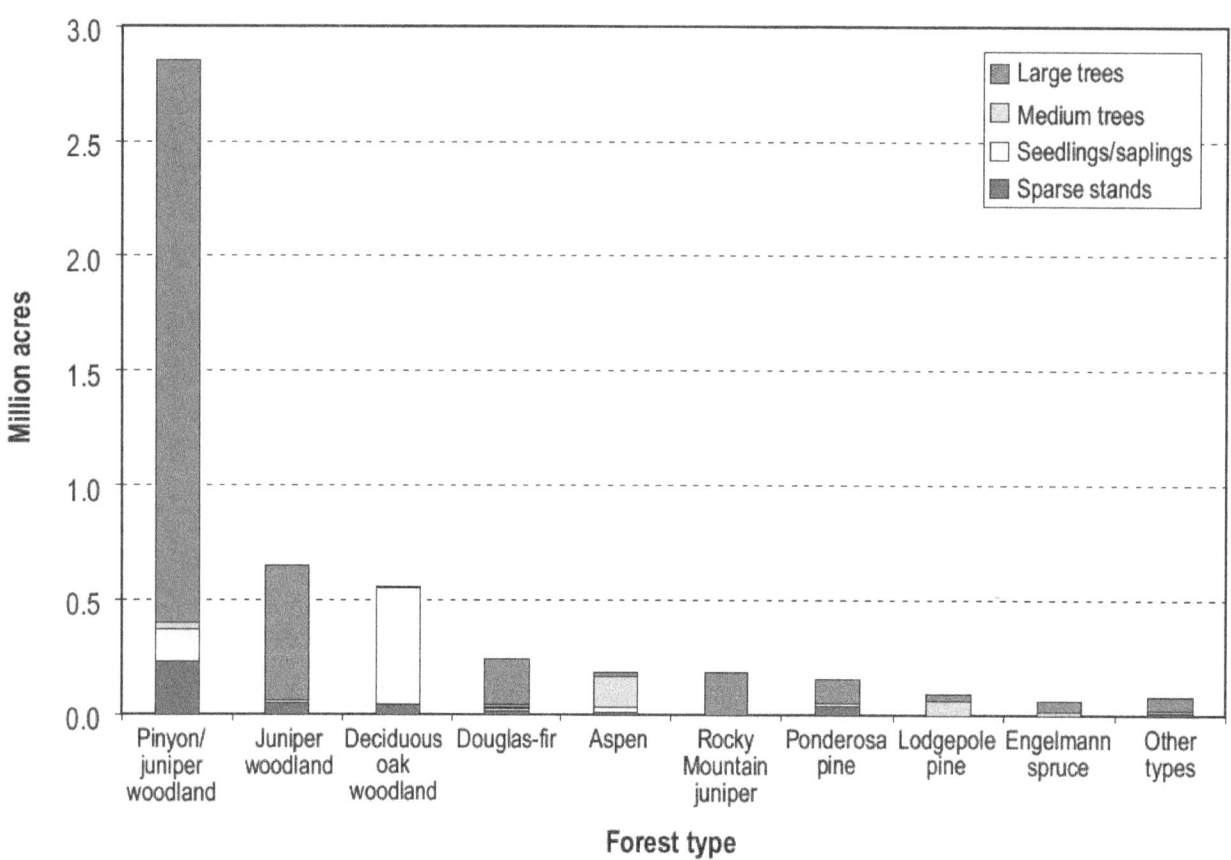

Figure CO 1 – Area of forest land by forest type and stand-size class, Colorado BLM land.

cubic feet, yielding net annual growth of 29 million cubic feet.

Figure CO 2 shows gross annual growth and mortality by species. "Other softwood" species that had recorded mortality were bristlecone pine, Engelmann spruce, and Rocky Mountain juniper. "Other hardwoods" with mortality were Gambel oak and Fremont or Rio Grande cottonwood. The only species with negative net annual growth were subalpine fir and Fremont or Rio Grande cottonwood. Seventy-four percent of the mortality in subalpine fir was caused by disease and 20 percent by fire. Mortality in the cottonwoods was all fire-related. Common pinyon had the largest mortality volume, 58 percent of which was caused by insects and 24 percent by fire. See Shaw et al., (2005) for a more detailed analysis of recent pinyon mortality. Overall, the largest cause of mortality was

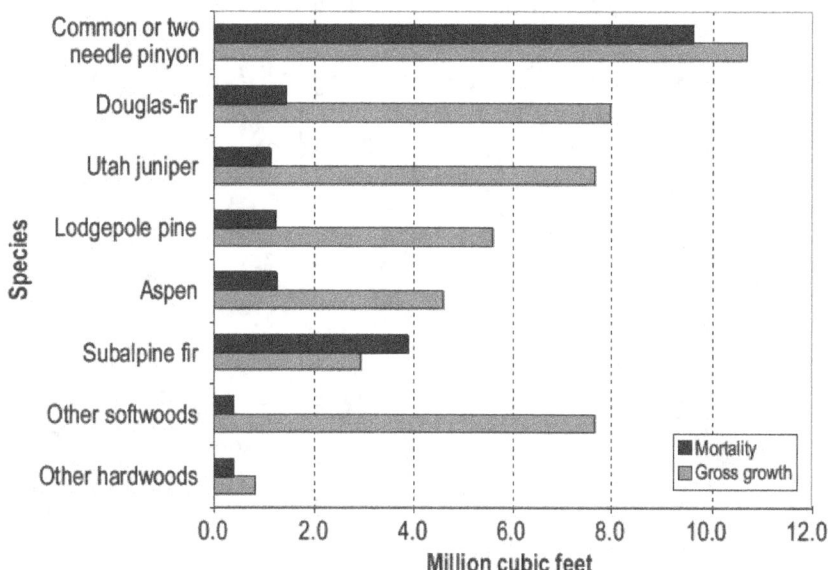

Figure CO 2 – Gross annual growth of all live trees 5.0 inches diameter and greater compared to mortality by species, Colorado BLM land.

insects, which contributed to 32 percent of all mortality. Insects were also the major cause of mortality in lodgepole pine (38 percent), in addition to common

pinyon. Fire caused 25 percent of the total mortality, and was the major cause in Utah juniper (91 percent) and Gambel oak (90 percent), as well as cottonwoods.

Idaho

The BLM manages over 12 million acres in Idaho and nearly 8 percent (945 thousand acres) is estimated to be forested. The largest portion of the forest land (28 percent) is in Douglas-fir forests, followed by western juniper forests with 23 percent and juniper woodlands with 15 percent. The area of forest land by forest type and stand-size class is displayed in Figure ID 1. Grand fir forests, with nearly 7 percent of the forest area (all are in the large-tree stand-size class), are the most significant forest type not described in Chapter 2 of this report. "Other types" in the figure include aspen forests, paper birch forests, pinyon/juniper woodland, subalpine fir forests, cottonwood, and whitebark pine forests.

Idaho data come from 2 years of annual data, collected in 2004 and 2005 by IW-FIA. This represents 20 percent of the annual grid that is sampled on a 10-year cycle. There were 38 forested conditions sampled, making each plot condition represent about 24,900 acres. Table ID1 lists estimates and standard errors for representative variables.

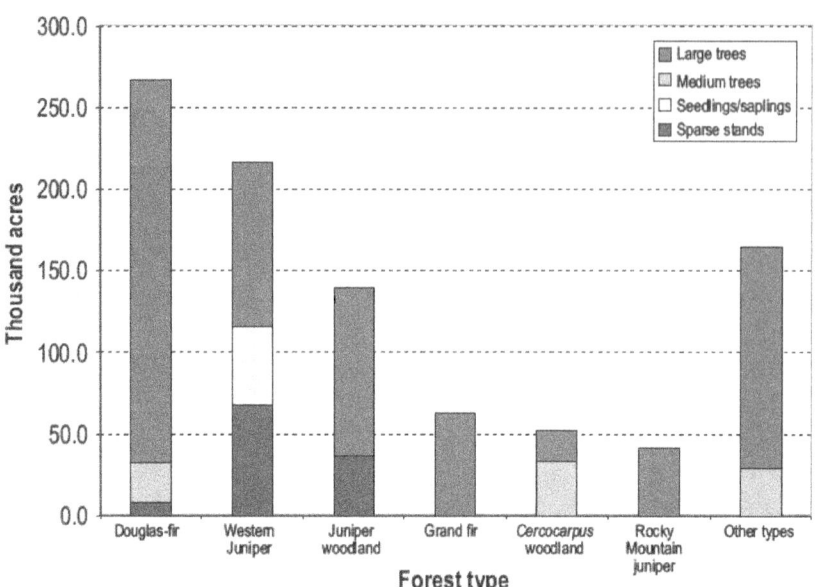

Figure ID 1 – Area of forest land by forest type and stand-size class, Idaho BLM land.

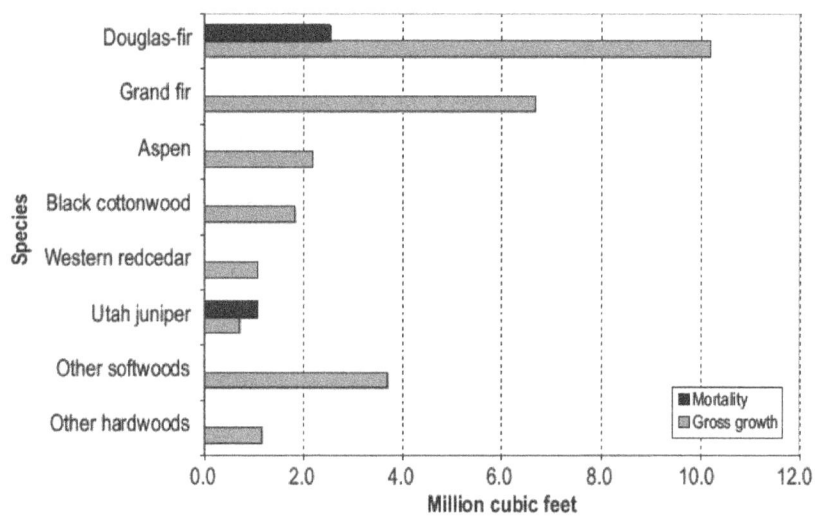

Figure ID 2 – Gross annual growth of all live trees 5.0 inches diameter and greater compared to mortality by species, Colorado BLM land.

Table ID 1. Percent standard error for area of forest land and net volume for all live trees on BLM land in Idaho.

Variable	Units	Estimate	Percent standard error
Forest land	Acres	945,309	± 17.05
Net live tree volume	Cubic feet	1,102,767,229	± 26.52

BLM forests in Idaho contain 1.1 billion net board feet in live tree wood volume. Net annual growth is estimated at 24 million cubic feet, based on a gross annual growth of 27.6 million cubic feet and an annual mortality of 3.6 million cubic feet. Gross annual growth and mortality by species are shown in

Figure ID 2. All of the mortality on BLM forests in Idaho was recorded in only two species: Douglas-fir and Utah juniper. Fifty-six percent of the Douglas-fir mortality was the result of disease, and 44 percent resulted from insect damage. Fire was the sole cause of all the recorded mortality in Utah junipers.

Montana (Including North Dakota and South Dakota)

The BLM manages 8 million acres in Montana, 59 thousand acres in North Dakota, and 274 thousand acres in South Dakota, for a total of 8.3 million acres. The BLM lands in all three States are managed by the BLM Montana State Office. Sixteen percent (1.3 million acres) of the land is forested.

The most common forest types are ponderosa pine forests, which cover 35 percent of the area, and Douglas-fir forests, which cover 33 percent. Figure MT 1 shows the area of forest land by forest type and stand-size class. "Other types" in the figure include mixed upland hardwoods, white spruce forests, bur oak, Engelmann spruce forests, and sugarberry/hackberry/elm/green ash forests. The most common forest types that are not discussed in Chapter 2 of this report are Engelmann spruce/subalpine fir forests and limber pine forests.

The data for Montana were collected on the annual grid by IW-FIA from 2003 to 2005. This accounts for 30 percent of the annual grid on a 10-year cycle. In North and South Dakota, annual data were collected by NC-FIA beginning in 2001, and the data used here include 2004 data, although data on BLM lands were not collected every year due to the small area and number of grid locations. The 4 years of data for North and South Dakota represent 80 percent of the annual grid on the NC-FIA 5-year cycle. The data were collected on a total of 87 forested conditions (81 in Montana and 3 each in North and South Dakota), so each plot condition represents about 15,200 acres. Table MT 1 shows estimates and standard errors for representative variables for Montana, and Tables ND 1 and SD 1 show the information for North Dakota and South Dakota, respectively. Note the higher standard errors where there are few plots.

Table MT 1. Percent standard error for area of forest land and net volume for all live trees on BLM land in Montana.

Variable	Units	Estimate	Percent standard error
Forest land	Acres	1,289,991	± 11.94
Net live tree volume	Cubic feet	1,476,735,046	± 17.92

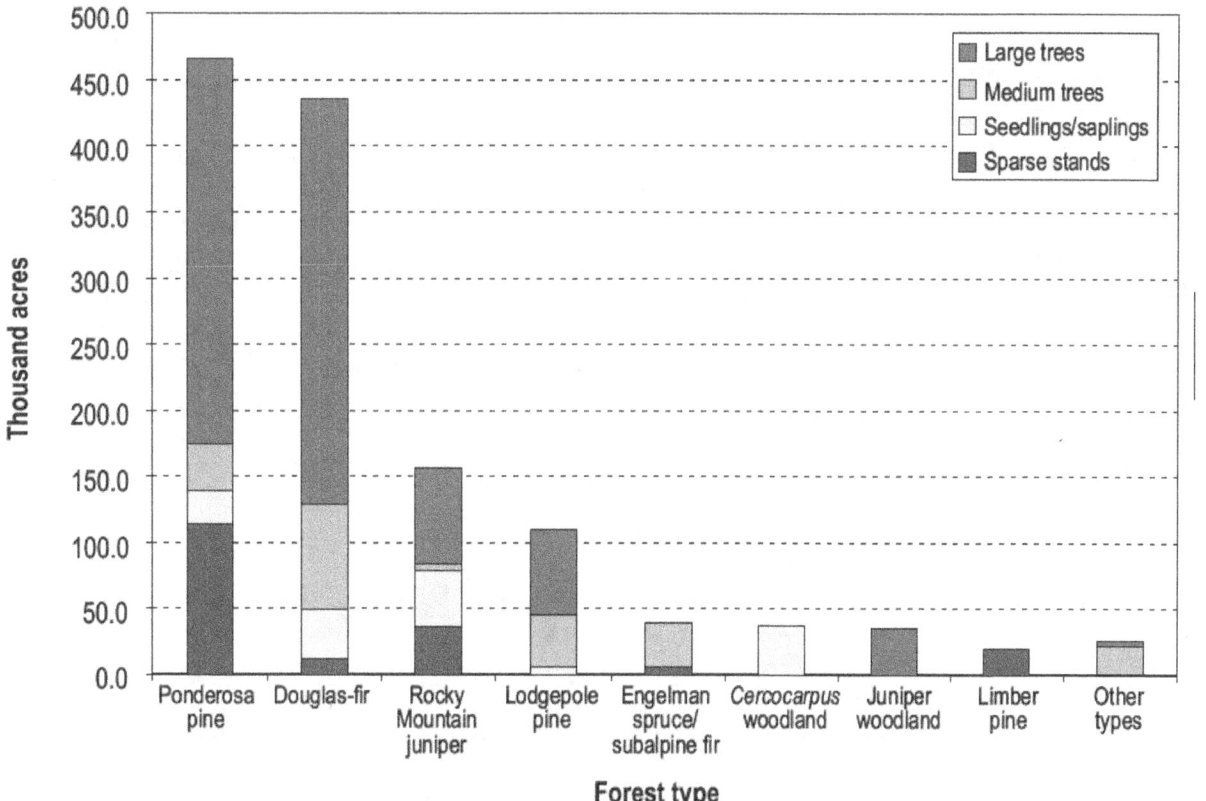

Figure MT 1 – Area of forest land by forest type and stand-size class, Montana BLM land including North Dakota and South Dakota State BLM data.

Table ND 1. Percent standard error for area of forest land and net volume for all live trees on BLM land in North Dakota.

Variable	Units	Estimate	Percent standard error
Forest land	Acres	10,369	± 74.63
Net live tree volume	Cubic feet	7,797,098	± 87.28

Table SD 1. Percent standard error for area of forest land and net volume for all live trees on BLM land in South Dakota.

Variable	Units	Estimate	Percent standard error
Forest land	Acres	25,394	± 55.72
Net live tree volume	Cubic feet	22,852,003	± 61.33

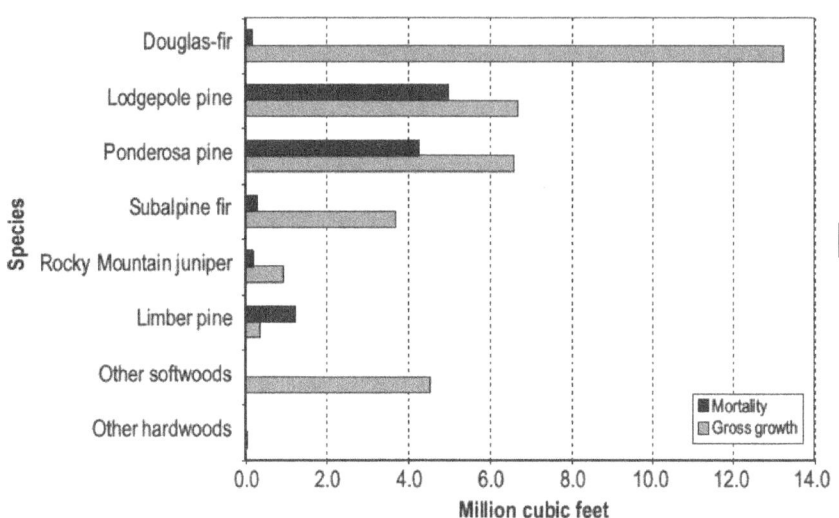

Figure MT 2 – Gross annual growth of all live trees 5.0 inches diameter and greater compared to mortality by species, Montana BLM land.

BLM forests and woodlands in Montana, North Dakota, and South Dakota contain 1.5 billion net cubic feet of live tree volume, 98 percent of which is in Montana. By forest type, the largest portion of the volume is in Douglas-fir forests (46 percent), followed by lodgepole pine forests and ponderosa pine forests (20 percent each). Also, by tree species, the greatest portion is in Douglas-fir trees (41 percent) followed by ponderosa pine trees (22 percent) and lodgepole pine trees (20 percent).

Since no data are available for growth and mortality in South Dakota or North Dakota, the following net growth information is for *Montana only*. Montana's gross annual growth on BLM land is estimated at 36 million cubic feet, while annual mortality is 11 million cubic feet, leading to a net annual growth of 25 million cubic feet. Figure MT 2 shows gross annual growth and mortality by species, and includes all species that had measured mortality. The species with the most mortality was lodgepole pine, in which mortality was 75 percent of gross growth. The only species with negative net annual growth was limber pine.

The overall leading cause of tree mortality in Montana BLM forests was fire, accounting for 69 percent of all mortality and contributing to mortality in lodgepole pine (71 percent), ponderosa pine (95 percent), and Rocky Mountain juniper (34 percent). Disease caused 13 percent of overall mortality, contributing to mortality in lodgepole pine (23 percent), ponderosa pine (5 percent), and limber pine (11 percent). While insects were a relatively minor cause of mortality overall, they contributed significantly to mortality in subalpine fir (76 percent) and Douglas-fir (100 percent). Other recorded mortality causes included weather-related events, vegetation (e.g., suppression, vines), and unknown causes.

Nevada

The BLM manages nearly 48 million acres in Nevada (the most BLM acreage in the contiguous States, second only to Alaska), of which 17 percent (7.8 million acres) is forested. The vast majority of the BLM forest land in Nevada (72 percent) is the pinyon/juniper woodland forest type, with an additional 21 percent as a juniper woodland forest type. The most common tall-stature forest type is white fir. Figure NV 1 shows the acreage of BLM forest land in Nevada by forest type and stand-size class.

Data for Nevada consist of 2 years of annual data collected in 2004 and 2005 by IW-FIA crews. IW-FIA States are on a 10-year annual cycle, so the data presented here represent 20 percent of the total FIA sampling grid for the State of Nevada. BLM forest land in Nevada was sampled on 303 conditions, making each plot condition represent about 25,800 acres. Table NV 1 displays standard errors for BLM forest land in Nevada for representative variables.

There are 3.6 billion net cubic feet of wood in all the live trees at least 5 inches diameter on BLM forest land in Nevada. Gross annual growth of all live trees

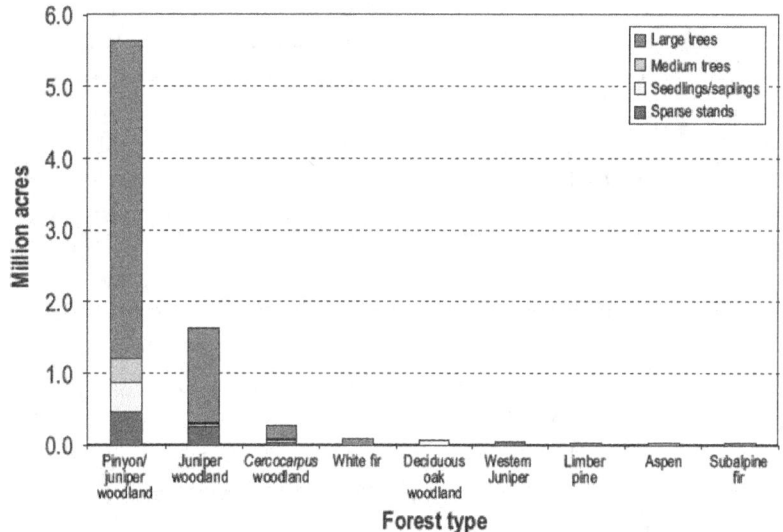

Figure NV 1 – Area of forest land by forest type and stand-size class, Nevada BLM land.

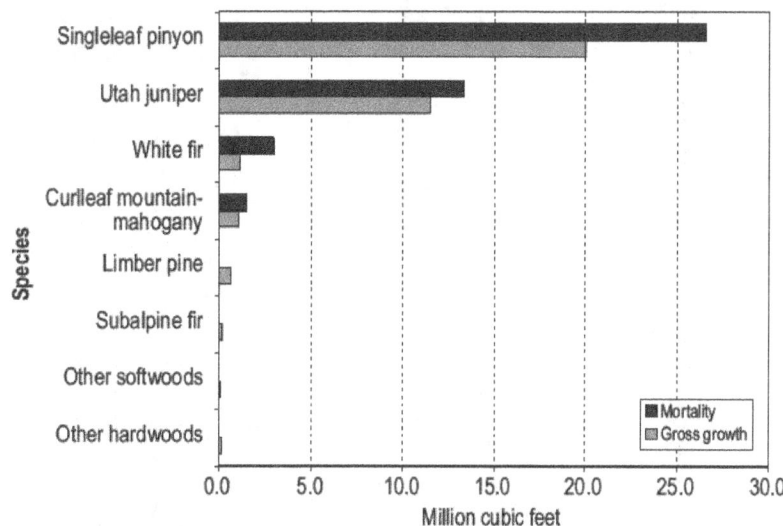

Figure NV 2 – Gross annual growth of all live trees 5.0 inches diameter and greater compared to mortality by species, Nevada BLM land.

Table NV 1. Percent standard error for area of forest land and net volume for all live trees on BLM land in Nevada.

Variable	Units	Estimate	Percent standard error
Forest land	Acres	7,831,219	± 4.61
Net live tree volume	Cubic feet	3,644,320,410	± 7.05

5 inches diameter and greater on Nevada BLM forest land is estimated at 34.9 million cubic feet, while the mortality estimate is 44.2 million cubic feet, for a negative net growth of 9.4 million cubic feet. The gross growth and mortality by species, including all of the species with mortality, is shown in Figure NV 2.

Generally speaking, most of the mortality in Nevada can be attributed to prolonged drought conditions over the last decade. More specifically, the leading

cause of mortality overall is fire, accounting for 51 percent of the mortality. However, on a species level, fire is the major agent of mortality only for Utah juniper, causing 95 percent of its mortality. For both singleleaf pinyon and white fir, the leading cause of mortality was insects, which led to 57 percent of the pinyon mortality, 59 percent of the white fir mortality, and 39 percent of the overall mortality. See Shaw et al. (2005) for a more detailed analysis of recent pinyon mortality.

New Mexico

Of the 13 million acres managed by the BLM in New Mexico, about 8 percent (1.1 million acres) is forested. The vast majority (84 percent) of the forests are pinyon/juniper woodlands, followed by juniper woodlands at 8 percent of the forest land. Ponderosa pine forests are the only tall-stature type, with 6 percent of the area forested. Figure NM 1 shows the area of forest land by forest type and stand-size class.

The data for New Mexico are from the periodic inventory finished in 2000 by IW-FIA. This inventory sampled most National Forests and timber forest types (tall-stature forests) from 1996 to 2000, and used data from the previous periodic inventory for most woodland type stands (O'Brien 2003). The previous inventory woodland plots include 77 percent of the plots on BLM land, which were sampled in 1986 and 1987 and used a plot design that did not have mapped conditions. The

remaining 23 percent of the plots were sampled in 1999 and 2000, and include all of the ponderosa pine forest and deciduous oak woodland plots, as well as some of the pinyon/juniper and juniper woodland plots. There were 177 forested condition proportions, resulting in an average of about 6,300 acres per sampled plot condition. Table NM 1 lists estimates and standard errors for representative variables.

Table NM 1. Percent standard error for area of forest land and net volume for all live trees on BLM land in New Mexico.

Variable	Units	Estimate	Percent standard error
Forest land	Acres	1,120,539	± 6.15
Net live tree volume	Cubic feet	541,087,075	± 7.88

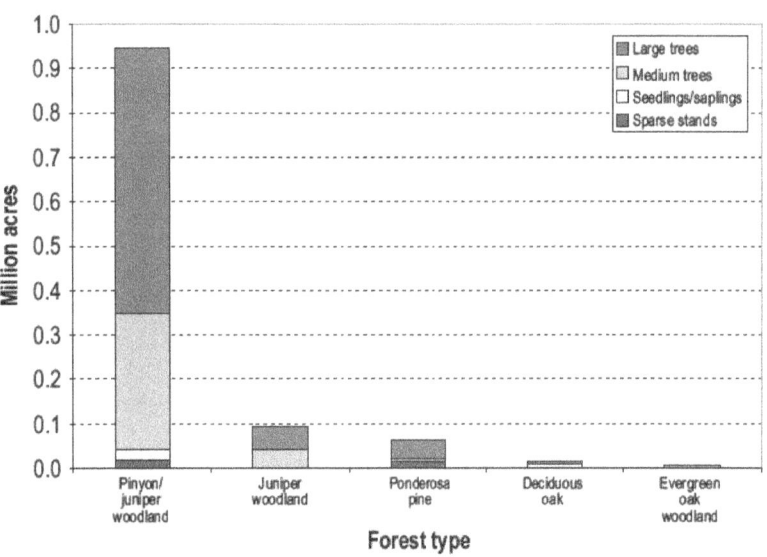

Figure NM 1 – Area of forest land by forest type and stand-size class, New Mexico BLM land.

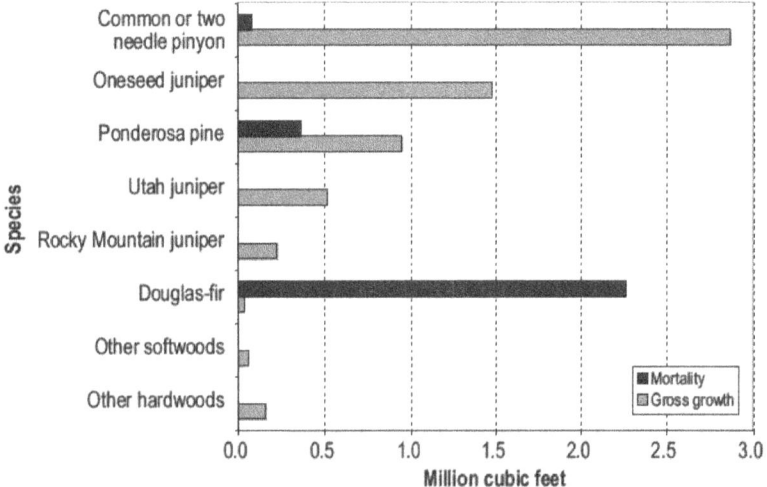

Figure NM 2 – Gross annual growth of all live trees 5.0 inches diameter and greater compared to mortality by species, New Mexico BLM land.

There are 514 million net cubic feet of wood volume in live trees 5 inches diameter or greater. Net annual growth is determined to be 3.6 million cubic feet, with gross annual growth of 6.3 million cubic feet and annual mortality of 2.7 million cubic feet. Figure NM 2 displays gross annual growth and mortality by species. Fire caused 93 percent of the mortality, including all of the mortality in Douglas-firs and 68 percent of that in ponderosa pines. Wind damage caused 32 percent of ponderosa pine mortality. All of the mortality in common pinyons was attributed to unknown causes. Because the data in New Mexico were collected prior to 2000, the recent insect mortality found in the surrounding States was not yet evident in New Mexico.

Oregon (Including Washington)

The BLM manages over 16 million acres of land in Oregon and 400 thousand acres in Washington. Twenty-three percent of this area (3.9 million acres) is estimated to be forested. The Pacific Coast States are much more diverse, in terms of forest types, than the Intermountain West States. To date, 21 different forest types have been recorded on BLM lands in Oregon and Washington by PNW-FIA. The most common of these is Douglas-fir (50 percent of the forest land), followed by western juniper (36 percent of the forest land). Figure OR 1 shows the area of forest land by forest type and stand-size class. "Other types" in the figure include canyon live oak/interior live oak, western hemlock, grand fir, white fir, bigleaf maple, *Cercocarpus* woodland, red alder, tanoak, aspen, sugar pine, western redcedar, western larch, red fir, and Port-Orford-cedar. Eighty-five percent of the forest area is included in the forest types discussed in Chapter 2 of this report, with the most important other types being Oregon white oak, Pacific madrone, and giant chinkapin (as shown in Figure OR 1).

The data for Oregon and Washington were collected by PNW-FIA crews from 2001 to 2004 in Oregon and 2002 to 2004 in Washington. This represents 40 percent and 30 percent, respectively, of the annual plots on a 10-year cycle. Three hundred forested conditions were sampled (295 in Oregon, 5 in Washington), so that each sampled plot condition represents an average of 12,900 acres (12,800 in Oregon, 15,800

in Washington). Table OR 1 lists estimates and standard errors for representative variables for Oregon, and Table WA 1 lists them for Washington. Note the high standard errors resulting from few plots in Washington.

BLM forests in Oregon and Washington are estimated to contain 12.4 billion cubic feet of net live volume, which is mostly in Douglas-fir. On a forest type basis, 75 percent of the volume is in Douglas-fir forests, with ponderosa pine forests the next largest contributor at 6 percent. On a species basis, 67 percent of the volume is in Douglas-fir trees and 6 percent in western hemlock. No data are currently available for growth and mortality in Oregon and Washington.

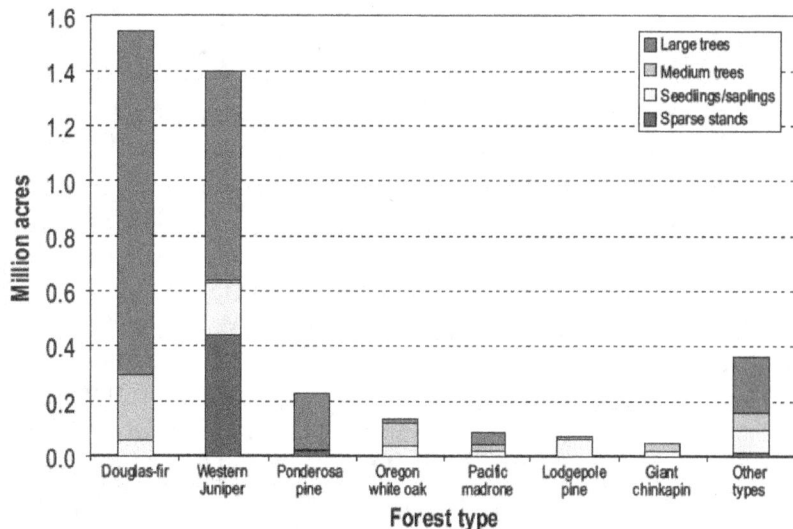

Figure OR 1 – Area of forest land by forest type and stand-size class, Oregon BLM land including Washington State BLM data.

Table OR 1. Percent standard error for area of forest land and net volume for all live trees on BLM land in Oregon.

Variable	Units	Estimate	Percent standard error
Forest land	Acres	3,788,679	± 4.38
Net live tree volume	Cubic feet	12,161,225,969	± 7.12

Table WA 1. Percent standard error for area of forest land and net volume for all live trees on BLM land in Washington.

Variable	Units	Estimate	Percent standard error
Forest land	Acres	78,826	± 47.47
Net live tree volume	Cubic feet	194,473,121	± 55.18

Utah

Of the nearly 23 million acres of land managed by the BLM in Utah, 34 percent (7.8 million acres) is forested. Two-thirds of the BLM forest land in Utah is pinyon/juniper woodlands, and about a quarter is juniper woodland. Figure UT 1 shows the distribution of BLM forest land in Utah by forest type and stand-size class. "Other types" in the figure include small acreages of aspen, limber pine, and subalpine fir forests and Intermountain maple woodland (bigtooth maple). The most common tall-stature forest type is Douglas-fir, followed by ponderosa pine.

Plots in Utah were sampled under the annual inventory by IW-FIA crews starting in 2000. The data cover 6 years, 2000 through 2005, and comprise 60 percent of the FIA annual sampling grid (10-year IW-FIA annual cycle). BLM forest land in Utah was sampled on 833 conditions, making the average area of forest land represented by a single plot condition about 9,400 acres. Table UT 1 displays standard errors for BLM forest land in Utah for representative variables.

Table UT 1. Percent standard error for area of forest land and net volume for all live trees on BLM land in Utah.

Variable	Units	Estimate	Percent standard error
Forest land	Acres	7,825,290	± 2.82
Net live tree volume	Cubic feet	4,397,494,022	± 4.12

Total net live volume of wood on BLM forests and woodlands in Utah is 4.0 billion cubic feet. Net annual growth on Utah BLM lands is estimated at 9.2

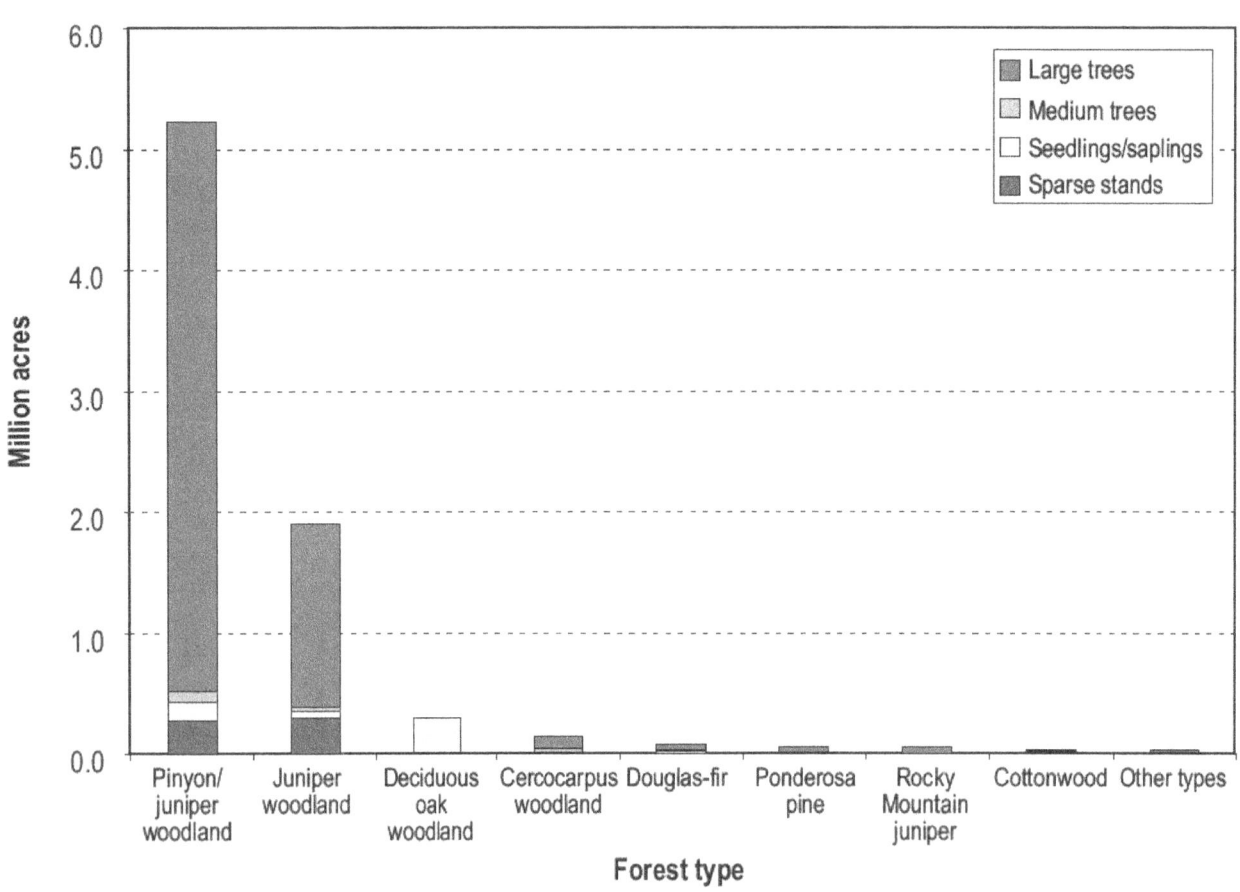

Figure UT 1 – Area of forest land by forest type and stand-size class, Utah BLM land.

million cubic feet, calculated from 33.2 million cubic feet of annual growth and 24.0 million cubic feet of mortality. The gross annual growth and mortality by species are shown in Figure UT 2. Smaller volumes of mortality were also measured for the "other softwoods," subalpine fir and Rocky Mountain juniper, and the "other hardwoods," curlleaf mountain-mahogany and Gambel oak. Species with negative net annual growth were Douglas-fir, ponderosa pine, subalpine fir, and white fir.

Fire was the major overall cause of mortality in Utah, causing 46 percent. Ninety percent or more of the mortality in Utah juniper, ponderosa pine, and white fir was fire-related, as was over 50 percent of Douglas-fir mortality. The only species with negative net growth, whose major cause of mortality was not fire, was subalpine fir, where all mortality was due to insect damage. Fifty percent of the mortality in common (twoneedle) pinyon was also due to insect damage, with fire, weather-related causes, and unknown causes contributing to the majority of the remaining mortality.

Mortality in singleleaf pinyon was caused primarily by disease (43 percent), with insects and unknown factors leading to about 25 percent each. See Shaw et al. (2005) for a more detailed analysis of recent pinyon mortality. Other minor factors contributing to overall mortality were animal activity and vegetation (e.g., competition, suppression, vines).

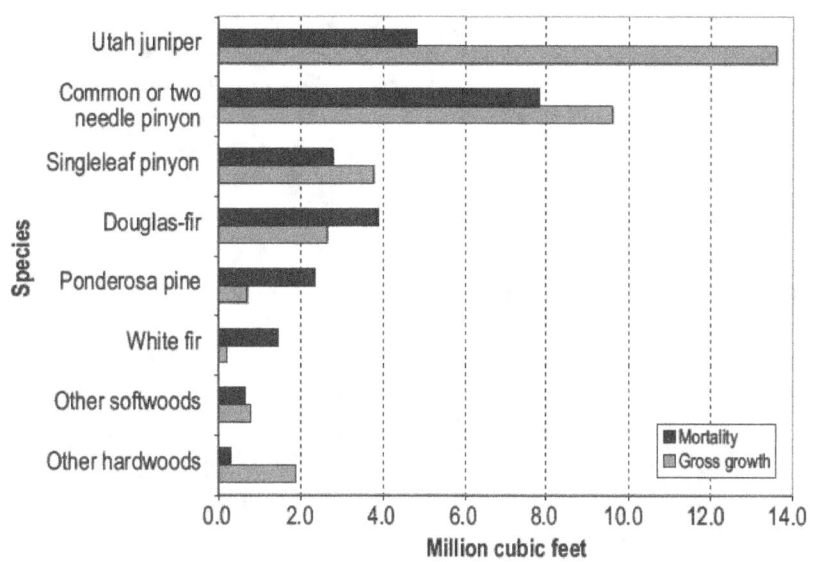

Figure UT 2 – Gross annual growth of all live trees 5.0 inches diameter and greater compared to mortality by species, Utah BLM land.

Wyoming

The BLM manages over 18 million acres in Wyoming, of which 7 percent (1.3 million acres) is forested. The most common forest type is juniper woodland (48 percent of the forested area), which, under periodic inventory procedures, includes woodlands that will be classified as Rocky Mountain juniper woodlands under annual inventory procedures. The next most common is limber pine forests (16 percent of the forest area), which is both the most common tall-stature forest and the most common type not described in Chapter 2 of this report. The area of forest land by forest type and stand-size class is shown in Figure WY 1. "Other

types" in the figure include pinyon/juniper woodlands, whitebark pine forests, sugarberry/hackberry/elm/green ash, cottonwood, and Engelmann spruce forests.

The data for Wyoming are from the last periodic inventory of that State, which was conducted by IW-FIA between 1998 and 2002 (Thompson et al. 2005). Most of the BLM lands were inventoried from 2000 to 2002. Periodic inventories sample 100 percent of the periodic grid. There were 245 forested condition proportions, resulting in an average of about 5,300 acres per sampled plot condition. Estimates and standard errors for representative variables are listed in table WY 1.

Table WY 1. Percent standard error for area of forest land and net volume for all live trees on BLM land in Wyoming.

Variable	Units	Estimate	Percent standard error
Forest land	Acres	1,290,162	± 6.04
Net live tree volume	Cubic feet	835,072,162	± 9.30

BLM forests in Wyoming contain 835 million net cubic feet of wood in live trees at least 5 inches diameter. Net annual growth is 10.9 million cubic feet, as determined by 18.4 million cubic feet of gross annual growth and 7.6 million cubic feet of annual mortality. Gross annual growth

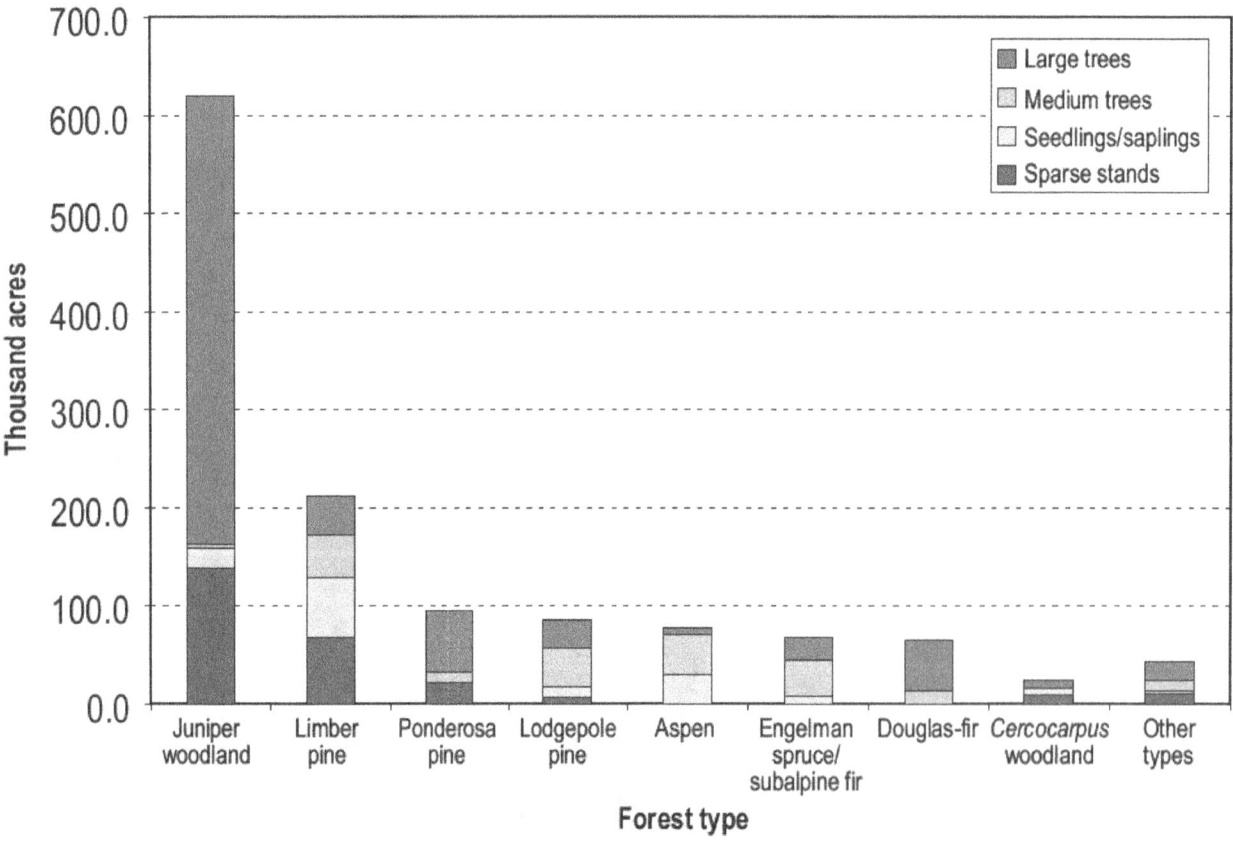

Figure WY 1 – Area of forest land by forest type and stand-size class, Wyoming BLM land.

and mortality by species are shown in Figure WY 2. The "other softwoods" with measured mortality were Utah and Rocky Mountain junipers. Douglas-fir trees had the most mortality (2.2 million cubic feet) and the largest proportional mortality (89 percent of gross growth). The major cause of mortality in Douglas-firs was insects, in this case identified as bark beetles (87 percent of Douglas-fir mortality). Insects were also the leading cause of overall mortality with 40 percent, and the major cause of mortality in ponderosa pines (72 percent) as well as Douglas-firs. Ninty-seven percent of insect damage was attributed to bark beetles.

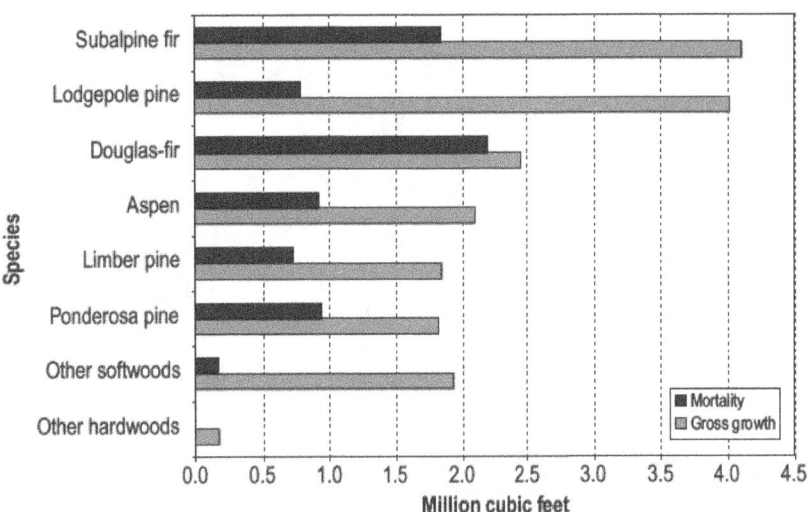

Figure WY 2 – Gross annual growth of all live trees 5.0 inches diameter and greater compared to mortality by species, Wyoming BLM land.

Diseases caused 27 percent of overall mortality, and were a major mortality cause in quaking aspen (93 percent), lodgepole pine (63 percent), and subalpine fir (31 percent). Diseases were broken out into several categories, with root diseases being the most significant, followed by cankers (in quaking aspens), dwarf mistletoe (in limber and lodgepole pines), and stem/butt rot (also in quaking aspens). Fires resulted in all of the Utah juniper mortality, 85 percent of the Rocky Mountain juniper mortality, and 28 percent of the ponderosa pine mortality. Weather, specified as wind damage, caused 45 percent of subalpine fir mortality. Other causes of mortality were suppression and unknown causes.

References Cited

Amman, G., McGregor, M., Cahill, D., and Klein, W. 1977. Guidelines for reducing losses of lodgepole pine to the mountain pine beetle in the Rocky Mountains. USDA Forest Service Gen. Tech. Rep. INT-36. Intermountain Forest and Range Exp. Sta., Ogden, UT. 22 pp.

Arner, S.L., Woudenberg, S., Waters, S., Vissage, J., MacLean, C., Thompson, M., and Hansen, M. 2001. National algorithms for determining stocking class, stand size class, and forest type for Forest Inventory and Analysis plots. Unpublished report on file at: U.S. Department of Agriculture, Forest Service, Rocky Mountain Research Station, Forestry Sciences Laboratory, Ogden, UT. 46 pp. Available online at *http://www.fs.fed.us/fmsc/fvs/documents/gtrs_arner.php*. Date accessed: December 15, 2006.

Bureau of Land Management. 2006. Public Land Statistics, 2005. Available online at *http://www.blm.gov/natacq/pls05/pls1-4_05.pdf*. Date accessed: December 15, 2006.

Gillespie, A.J.R. 1999. Rationale for a national annual forest inventory program. Journal of Forestry. 97(12):16-20.

Helms, J.A. (ed.). 1998a. The Dictionary of Forestry. Bethesda, MD: The Society of American Foresters, p. 71.

____ 1998b. The Dictionary of Forestry. Bethesda, MD: The Society of American Foresters, p. 40.

O'Brien, R.A. 2003. New Mexico's Forest Resources, 2000. Resour. Bull. RMRS-RB-3. Fort Collins, CO: U.S. Department of Agriculture, Forest Service, Rocky Mountain Research Station. 117 pp. Available online at *http://www.fs.fed.us/rm/ogden/pdfs/rmrs_rb003.pdf*. Date accessed: December 15, 2006.

Reineke, L.H. 1933. Perfecting a stand-density index for even-aged forests. Journal of Agricultural Research 46:627-638.

Shaw, J.D. 2000. Application of stand density index to irregularly structure stands. Western Journal of Applied Forestry 15:40-42.

Shaw, J.D, Steed, B., and DeBlander, L.T. 2005. Forest Inventory and Analysis (FIA) annual inventory answers the question: what is happening to pinyon-juniper woodlands? Journal of Forestry 103(6):280-285.

Thompson, M.T., DeBlander, L.T., and Blackard, J.A. 2005. Wyoming's Forests, 2002. Resour. Bull. RMRS-RB-6. Fort Collins, CO: U.S. Department of Agriculture, Forest Service, Rocky Mountain Research Station. 148 pp. Available online at *http://www.fs.fed.us/rm/ogden/pdfs/wyoming_state.pdf*. Date accessed: December 15, 2006.

U.S. Department of Agriculture, Forest Service. 2005a. Forest inventory and analysis national core field guide, volume 1: field data collection procedures for phase 2 plots, version 3.0. U.S. Department of Agriculture, Forest Service, Washington Office. Internal report. On file with: U.S. Department of Agriculture, Forest Service, Forest Inventory and Analysis, Rosslyn Plaza, 1620 North Kent Street, Arlington, VA 22209. Available online at *http://socrates.lv-hrc.nevada.edu/fia/index.htm*. Date accessed: December 15, 2006.

____ 2005b. Forest Vegetation Simulator. Available at *http://www.fs.fed.us/fmsc/fvs*. Date accessed: December 15, 2006. FHTET mountain pine beetle FVS extensions available online at *http://www.fs.fed.us/foresthealth/technology/fvsemap/mb_rating.html*. Date accessed: December 15, 2006.

Glossary

Basal area is the cross-sectional area, in square feet, of the bole of a tree at the point where diameter is measured, including the bark. Basal area is a common indicator of stand tree density. It is calculated for this report on all live trees of 1-inch diameter and larger, and is reported as basal area per acre.

Biomass is the oven-dry weight, in tons, of wood fiber in all live trees 1-inch diameter and larger. Biomass for this report includes the bole, bark, and branches, but not foliage. Volume and biomass will be reported for all types, but the focus for discussion of the amount of wood fiber will be biomass for woodlands and volume for forests.

Diameter at breast height (DBH) is the diameter of a tree, measured at 4.5 feet (1.37 m) above the ground (breast height) on the uphill side of a tree. The point of diameter measurement may vary on abnormally formed trees.

Diameter at root collar (DRC) is the diameter of a tree (usually a woodland species) measured outside the bark at the ground line or root collar.

Gross annual growth is the net annual sound cubic-foot growth of live trees in the last year. In the annual inventory, this will be determined by measuring the same trees in every cycle and comparing the measurements from the previous cycle. Since all of the States with BLM forests are in the first annual cycle, data from

this method is not yet available. IW-FIA uses an "interim" method for estimating growth, where shallow core samples are taken from some trees on the plot. The width of the last 10 years of growth is averaged for a yearly estimate of growth. All cores taken for stand age determination also have the last 10 years of growth measured. The other FIA units have not established interim measures of tree growth, so precise data will not be available until the second annual cycle.

Mortality is the net cubic-foot volume of trees that have died in the last year. In the annual inventory, this will be determined by measuring the same trees in every cycle and recording dead trees that were alive at the previous cycle. Since all of the States with BLM forests are in the first annual cycle, data from this method is not yet available. IW-FIA uses an "interim" method for estimating mortality, where crews record mortality data for trees that are estimated to have died within the past 5 years, using species-specific criteria for time-since-death estimates. The other FIA units have not established interim measures of tree mortality, so precise data will not be available until the second annual cycle.

Net annual growth is the difference between gross annual growth and mortality. It is an indicator of forest health and vigor. In annual inventory cycles subsequent to the first, tree removals will also be measured and subtracted from gross growth.

Snags (see standing dead trees).

Stand age is the average age of the trees in the predominant stand-size class of the stand. In FIA, stand age is estimated from tree cores from a few selected trees of each species and size class on the plot. More trees are core-sampled in dense stands than in sparse stands. In some cases, trees in the stand, but not sampled on the plot, may be cored for stand age. Many other factors can also influence the number of trees available for determining stand age. For purposes of this report, stand age is presented in 50-year or 25-year age classes. Sparse stands have a reported age of "unavailable," as do a few other stands where aging was not possible for various reasons.

Stand Density Index (SDI) is an index of relative stand density based on the number of trees per acre and their mean size (Reineke 1933). The SDI figure represents density in terms of the number of trees per acre at an average stand diameter of 10 inches DBH. In even-aged stands, SDI can be calculated using the quadratic mean diameter (Dq) (Reineke 1933):

$$SDI_{Dq} = TPA * (Dq/10)^{1.6}$$

SDI can also be calculated using the diameter of individual trees or the mid-point of the diameter class of groups of trees (summation method) (Shaw 2000):

$$SDI_{sum} = \Sigma(TPA_j * (D_j/10)^{1.6})$$

where D_j is the diameter (in

inches) of the jth tree in the sample, and TPA_j is the number of trees represented by the jth tree. The summation method can be modified to where Dj represents the mid-point of diameter class j and TPA_j is the number of trees per acre in that diameter class. All SDIs for individual trees or groups would be added to determine the SDI of the stand. This is the preferred method for calculating SDI for uneven-aged and two-storied stands.

In even-aged stands, SDI is similar when calculated using the two methods, but the methods produce increasingly different results as stand structure becomes more irregular (Shaw 2000). Because FIA plots cover all stand structures, SDI is calculated by summation in FIA reporting. In FIA calculations, TPA_j is is the FIA variable TPACURR and D_j is the FIA variable DIA.

Maximum SDI (SDI_max) is the highest possible realitive density for a given species or, in the case of mixed-species forest types, the maximum for stands that meet the type definition. Each species or type has its own maximum SDI, which is essentially independent of site quality and stand age. Relative density can be expressed as a percent of a species' or forest types' maximum SDI (%SDI $_{max}$). These %SDI$_{max}$ correspond to silviculturally important threshholds in realtive density:

100 %SDI$_{max}$ Maximum SDI (theoretical maximum combination of mean size and density)
60 %SDI$_{max}$ Lower limit of self thinning zone
35 %SDI$_{max}$ Lower limit of full site occupancy
25%SDI$_{max}$ Onset of competition

SDI is reported based on these thresholds. SDI maximum values are defined as the 98th percentile of the distribution of SDIs in all FIA plots classified in each forest type. Table 1 lists SDI maximum values for the 10 types discussed in this report. In the SDI calculations, DBH is used for tall-stature species and DRC is used for low-stature species.

The values in Table 1 should be used consistently with the methods used to calculate SDI at the stand level. Because FIA calculates SDI by summation, the summation maximum values (SDI$_{sum}$) are used as reference values in this report. The Dq-based maximum values (SDI$_{Dq}$) are provided for comparison.

Stand size is a categorization of forest land based on the predominant diameter size of live trees contributing to the stocking of a stand. Diameter is taken at breast height (DBH) for forest (tall-stature) species and at the root collar (DRC) for woodland (low-stature) species. Large diameter trees are hardwoods at least 11 inches in diameter and softwoods and low stature species at least 9 inches in diameter. Medium diameter trees are at least 5 inches in diameter, but smaller than large trees and saplings/seedlings are less than 5 inches in diameter

(seedlings are less than 1 inch diameter). Sparsely stocked stands are primarily those that have recently been affected by large-scale disturbance, such as harvest or fire, but may include stands with very low tree density (less than 10 percent stocking) for various other reasons.

Standing dead trees (snags) are an important component of forest ecosystems, especially in terms of wildlife habitat. Many animals are dependent upon snags, but the species, size, and density of snags required for quality habitat varies according to the wildlife species. In general, larger snags are less common relative to smaller snags. Dead trees may remain standing long after they have died, so the number of snags does not necessarily reflect an estimate of recent mortality.

Volume refers to wood volume, in cubic feet, in the merchantable bole of all live trees 5 inches diameter and larger. Volume for this report is calculated on the net volume per tree, and does not include rotten, missing, or form cull portions. Volume and biomass will be reported for all types, but the focus for discussion of the amount of wood fiber will be biomass for woodlands and volume for forests.

Table 1. SDI maximum values for common BLM forest types.

FIA Code	Forest Type	Maximum SDI$_{sum}$	Maximum SDI$_{Dq}$
182	Rocky Mountain juniper	377	416
183	Western juniper	317	377
184	Juniper woodland	386	419
185	Pinyon-juniper woodland	370	425
201	Douglas-fir	484	557
221	Ponderosa pine	377	452
281	Lodgepole pine	532	579
901	Aspen	488	527
925	Deciduous oak woodland	476	512
953	Cercocarpus woodland	416	457

Appendix A
Data Tables

Data Table PJ 1 -- Area of pinyon/juniper woodland by trees-per-acre class and State, BLM land, 2005.

	State								All states
Trees/acre	AZ	CA	CO	ID	NV	NM	UT	WY	
	- - - - - - - - - - Thousand acres - - - - - - - - - -								
< 100	347	207	652	--	1,597	374	1,855	17	5,049
100 - 199	328	38	730	--	1,244	297	1,446	--	4,084
200 - 299	187	59	465	--	957	136	815	--	2,619
300 - 399	64	--	396	--	746	50	448	--	1,703
400 - 499	13	--	182	--	347	42	303	--	886
500 - 599	51	--	166	--	244	15	126	--	602
600 - 699	13	--	53	29	256	16	104	--	471
700 - 799	13	--	59	--	125	6	39	--	242
800 - 899	--	--	49	--	31	5	19	--	105
900 - 999	--	--	35	--	52	--	29	--	116
1000 +	--	--	65	--	46	5	43	--	159
All classes	1,015	303	2,852	29	5,644	946	5,227	17	16,035

Data Table PJ 2 -- Area of pinyon/juniper woodland by State and stand-size class, BLM land, 2005.

	Stand-size class				
State	Sparse stands (<10% stocked)	Seedlings/saplings (0-4.9" dbh/drc)	Medium trees (5-9" or 5-11" dbh/drc)	Large trees (9 or 11"+ dbh/drc)	Total
	- - - - - - - - - - Thousand acres - - - - - - - - - -				
Arizona	137	90	37	751	1,015
California	94	48	14	148	303
Colorado	232	141	32	2,447	2,852
Idaho	--	--	--	29	29
Nevada	461	410	334	4,440	5,644
New Mexico	19	24	306	598	946
Utah	280	156	88	4,703	5,227
Wyoming	6	--	--	11	17
All states	1,229	869	811	13,126	16,035

Data Table PJ 3 -- Area of pinyon/juniper woodland by stand-age class and State, BLM land, 2005.

| Stand-age class | State | | | | | | | | All states |
	AZ	CA	CO	ID	NV	NM	UT	WY	
	- - - - - - - - - - Thousand acres - - - - - - - - -								
Unavailable	137	94	232	--	461	27	280	6	1,237
1 - 50 years	90	--	157	--	503	112	164	--	1,025
51 - 100 years	261	147	299	29	1,387	514	738	6	3,382
101 - 150 years	216	62	575	--	1,339	163	1,459	5	3,817
151 - 200 years	162	--	1,033	--	1,341	106	1,385	--	4,026
201 - 250 years	88	--	420	--	356	13	675	--	1,553
251 - 300 years	49	--	100	--	175	12	282	--	618
301 - 350 years	3	--	18	--	83	--	163	--	268
351 - 400 years	--	--	18	--	--	--	40	--	58
401 - 450 years	9	--	--	--	--	--	20	--	29
Over 450 years	--	--	--	--	--	--	20	--	20
All ages	1,015	303	2,852	29	5,644	946	5,227	17	16,035

Data Table PJ 4 -- Area of pinyon/juniper woodland by live-tree basal area class and State, BLM land, 2005.

| Basal area class (ft^2/acre) | State | | | | | | | | All states |
	AZ	CA	CO	ID	NV	NM	UT	WY	
	- - - - - - - - - - Thousand acres - - - - - - - - - -								
0 - 25	238	128	334	--	875	126	558	6	2,265
26 - 50	219	90	193	--	1,125	224	778	--	2,629
51 - 75	185	41	401	--	1,029	181	996	--	2,833
76 - 100	156	--	376	--	1,026	174	871	--	2,603
101 - 125	88	15	421	--	659	136	631	5	1,955
126 - 150	88	17	242	29	433	55	561	--	1,425
151 - 175	26	12	464	--	193	20	334	6	1,054
176 - 200	3	--	155	--	153	15	263	--	589
201 - 225	--	--	99	--	59	16	131	--	305
226 - 250	--	--	43	--	31	--	56	--	130
251 - 300	13	--	108	--	31	--	16	--	168
301 +	--	--	16	--	31	--	31	--	78
All classes	1,015	303	2,852	29	5,644	946	5,227	17	16,035

Data Table PJ 5 -- Area of pinyon/juniper woodland by State and percent stand density index (SDI), BLM land, 2005.

| State | Percent of maximum SDI | | | | Total |
	< 25	25.0 - 34.9	35.0 - 59.9	60 +	
	- - - - - - - - - - Thousand acres - - - - - - - - - -				
Arizona	444	223	269	80	1,015
California	247	12	44	--	303
Colorado	560	343	909	1,039	2,852
Idaho	--	--	--	29	29
Nevada	1,978	796	1,896	974	5,644
New Mexico	392	134	337	83	946
Utah	1,568	949	1,580	1,131	5,227
Wyoming	6	--	11	--	17
All states	5,195	2,457	5,046	3,337	16,035

Data Table PJ 6 -- Number of standing dead trees on pinyon/juniper woodlands by species and diameter class, BLM land, 2005.

| Species | Diameter class (inches) | | | All classes |
	5.0-10.9	11.0-18.9	19.0+	
	- - - - - - - - - - Thousand trees - - - - - - - - - -			
White fir	225	--	--	225
Alligator juniper	--	33	--	33
Utah juniper	45,469	36,007	7,586	89,062
Rocky Mountain juniper	686	1,230	297	2,213
Oneseed juniper	636	894	168	1,698
Common pinyon	26,999	12,822	442	40,263
Ponderosa pine	--	--	56	56
Singleleaf pinyon	40,499	10,785	853	52,137
Arizona pinyon pine	--	70	--	70
Douglas-fir	624	477	207	1,308
Softwood total	115,138	62,318	9,609	187,065
Curlleaf mountain-mahogany	5,465	981	186	6,632
Gambel oak	588	--	43	631
Hardwood total	6,053	981	229	7,263
All species	121,191	63,299	9,838	194,329

Data Table CJW 1 -- Area of combined juniper woodland by trees-per-acre class and State, BLM land, 2005.

Trees/acre	State											All States
	AZ	CA	CO	ID	MT	NV	NM	ND	UT	WY	
	- - - - - - - Thousand acres - - - - - -											
< 100	416	105	334	100	82	991	81	--	1,336	298	3,742
100 - 199	63	17	261	--	56	375	6	--	385	169	1,332
200 - 299	13	--	155	24	--	239	--	--	116	64	610
300 - 399	3	--	34	29	--	21	--	2	33	27	149
400 - 499	12	--	--	--	13	--	--	--	9	16	50
500 - 599	13	--	15	29	--	--	--	--	30	17	105
600 - 699	--	--	--	--	--	--	--	--	10	--	10
700 - 799	--	--	--	--	--	--	--	--	10	--	10
800 - 899	--	--	--	--	17	--	--	--	10	7	34
900 - 999	--	--	18	--	--	--	6	--	--	10	33
1000 +	--	14	21	--	22	--	--	--	9	12	77
All classes	520	137	838	181	189	1,626	92	2	1,949	619	6,153

Data Table CJW 2 -- Area of combined juniper woodland by State and stand-size class, BLM land, 2005.

State	Stand-size class				Total
	Sparse stands (<10% stocked)	Seedlings/saplings (0-4.9" dbh/drc)	Medium trees (5-9" or 5-11" dbh/drc)	Large trees (9 or 11"+ dbh/drc)	
	- - - - - - - - - - Thousand acres - - - - - - - - - -				
Arizona	125	12	--	383	520
California	77	14	--	46	137
Colorado	52	12	--	774	838
Idaho	36	--	--	145	181
Montana	36	43	5	105	189
Nevada	254	25	29	1,318	1,626
New Mexico	--	--	41	51	92
North Dakota	--	--	--	2	2
Utah	300	51	41	1,557	1,949
Wyoming	138	21	4	456	619
All states	1,019	178	120	4,836	6,153

Data Table CJW 3 -- Area of combined juniper woodland by stand-age class and State, BLM land, 2005.

Stand-age class	State										All states
	AZ	CA	CO	ID	MT	NV	NM	ND	UT	WY	
	- - - - - - - Thousand acres - - - - - - -										
Unavailable	125	88	52	36	36	254	--	--	300	138	1,031
1 - 50 years	12	31	25	--	50	25	11	--	73	50	278
51 - 100 years	121	17	89	53	50	302	56	2	490	202	1,382
101 - 150 years	89	--	174	12	53	375	6	--	490	102	1,302
151 - 200 years	26	--	364	22	--	447	18	--	348	90	1,314
201 - 250 years	123	--	100	58	--	115	--	--	125	24	545
251 - 300 years	12	--	21	--	--	108	--	--	100	6	247
301 - 350 years	--	--	12	--	--	--	--	--	19	6	37
351 - 400 years	12	--	--	--	--	--	--	--	5	--	17
All ages	520	137	838	181	189	1,626	92	2	1,949	619	6,153

Data Table CJW 4 -- Area of combined juniper woodland by live-tree basal area class and State, BLM land, 2005.

Basal area class (ft²/acre)	State										All states
	AZ	CA	CO	ID	MT	NV	NM	ND	UT	WY	
	- - - - - - - - - - Thousand acres - - - - - - - - - -										
0 - 25	217	77	96	36	81	370	18	--	636	157	1,688
26 - 50	138	31	57	51	46	450	45	2	481	122	1,423
51 - 75	91	17	133	36	7	379	12	--	283	97	1,056
76 - 100	26	12	107	--	--	170	--	--	152	63	528
101 - 125	36	--	158	--	5	149	11	--	124	56	539
126 - 150	12	--	70	29	--	51	--	--	106	32	300
151 - 175	--	--	15	--	37	7	--	--	50	28	138
176 - 200	--	--	65	--	--	29	6	--	21	28	148
201 - 225	--	--	66	--	--	--	--	--	35	20	121
226 - 250	--	--	16	29	--	--	--	--	28	--	73
251 - 300	--	--	31	--	13	21	--	--	25	10	100
301 +	--	--	22	--	--	--	--	--	11	6	39
All classes	520	137	838	181	189	1,626	92	2	1,949	619	6,153

Data Table CJW 5 -- Area of combined juniper woodland by State and percent stand density index (SDI), BLM land, 2005.

State	\< 25	25.0 - 34.9	35.0 - 59.9	60 +	Total
		- - - - - - - - - - *Thousand acres* - - - - - - - - - -			
Arizona	382	65	73	--	520
California	111	12	14	--	137
Colorado	231	79	292	237	838
Idaho	100	24	29	29	181
Montana	127	2	30	29	189
Nevada	966	243	344	72	1,626
New Mexico	69	6	11	6	92
North Dakota	2	--	--	--	2
Utah	1,275	186	311	177	1,949
Wyoming	292	91	121	116	619
All states	3,553	707	1,226	666	6,153

Data Table CJW 6 -- Number of standing dead trees on combined juniper woodlands by species and diameter class, BLM land, 2005.

Species	Diameter class (inches)			All classes
	5.0-10.9	11.0-18.9	19.0+	
	- - - - - - - - *Thousand trees* - - - - - - - -			
Redberry juniper	--	71	--	71
California juniper	569	219	17	805
Utah juniper	22,343	14,087	1,852	38,283
Rocky Mountain juniper	2,813	662	453	3,928
Oneseed juniper	377	209	59	645
Common pinyon	1,071	313	--	1,384
Limber pine	212	78	--	290
Ponderosa pine	204	287	--	491
Singleleaf pinyon	218	218	--	436
Douglas-fir	35	--	--	35
Softwood total	27,842	16,145	2,381	46,368
Curlleaf mountain-mahogany	249	--	--	249
Narrowleaf cottonwood	56	38	--	94
Gambel oak	369	--	--	369
Hardwood total	673	38	--	711
All species	28,515	16,183	2,381	47,079

Data Table C-DF 1 -- Area of Coastal Douglas-fir forest by trees-per-acre class and State, BLM land, 2005.

Trees/acre	State California	State Oregon	All states
	- - - - - - - - - Thousand acres - - - - - - - - -		
< 100	--	183	183
100 - 199	--	401	401
200 - 299	17	360	377
300 - 399	--	215	215
400 - 499	--	110	110
500 - 599	--	19	19
600 - 699	--	14	14
700 - 799	--	66	66
800 - 899	--	58	58
900 - 999	--	--	--
1000 +	--	53	53
All classes	17	1,480	1,497

Data Table C-DF 2 -- Area of Coastal Douglas-fir forest by State and stand-size class, BLM land, 2005.

State	Stand-size class Sparse stands (<10% stocked)	Stand-size class Seedlings/saplings (0-4.9" dbh/drc)	Stand-size class Medium trees (5-9" or 5-11" dbh/drc)	Stand-size class Large trees (9 or 11"+ dbh/drc)	Total
	- - - - - - - - - - Thousand acres - - - - - - - - - -				
California	--	--	--	17	17
Oregon	--	58	226	1,196	1,480
All states	--	58	226	1,213	1,497

Data Table C-DF 3 -- Area of Coastal Douglas-fir forest by stand-age class and State, BLM land, 2005.

Stand-age class	State California	State Oregon	All states
	- - - - - - Thousand acres - - - - - -		
Unavailable	--	--	--
1 - 50 years	--	604	604
51 - 100 years	17	434	451
101 - 150 years	--	207	207
151 - 200 years	--	45	45
201 - 250 years	--	146	146
251 - 300 years	--	30	30
Over 300 years	--	14	14
All ages	17	1,480	1,497

Data Table C-DF 4 -- Area of Coastal Douglas-fir forest by live-tree basal area

Basal area class (ft²/acre)	State		All states
	California	Oregon	
	- - - - - - - - Thousand acres - - - - - - - -		
0 - 25	--	11	11
26 - 50	--	57	57
51 - 75	--	130	130
76 - 100	--	124	124
101 - 125	--	43	43
126 - 150	17	189	205
151 - 175	--	219	219
176 - 200	--	135	135
201 - 225	--	129	129
226 - 250	--	117	117
251 - 275	--	97	97
276 - 300	--	109	109
301 - 400	--	108	108
401 +	--	12	12
Total	17	1,480	1,497

Data Table C-DF 5 -- Area of Coastal Douglas-fir forest by State and percent stand density index (SDI), BLM land, 2005.

State	Percent of maximum SDI				Total
	< 25	25.0 - 34.9	35.0 - 59.9	60 +	
	- - - - - - - - - - Thousand acres - - - - - - - - - -				
California	--	--	17	--	17
Oregon	146	85	654	594	1,480
All states	146	85	671	594	1,497

Data Table C-DF 6 -- Number of standing dead trees on Coastal Douglas-fir forests by species and diameter class, BLM land, 2005.

	Diameter class (inches)			
	5.0-	11.0-		All
Species	10.9	18.9	19.0+	classes
	- - - - - - - - Thousand trees - - - - - - - -			
Grand fir	166	--	--	166
California red fir	--	--	12	12
Port-Orford-cedar	--	--	16	16
Incense-cedar	83	71	22	177
Sugar pine	83	--	61	144
Ponderosa pine	83	133	151	368
Douglas-fir	10,398	3,871	2,860	17,129
Western redcedar	71	--	20	91
Western hemlock	1,301	332	--	1,633
Mountain hemlock	98	--	--	98
Softwood total	12,284	4,408	3,143	19,834
Bigleaf maple	293	--	--	293
Red alder	688	71	--	759
Pacific madrone	1,547	509	83	2,139
Giant chinkapin, golden chinkapin	83	--	--	83
Tanoak	514	--	--	514
Bitter cherry	133	--	--	133
Canyon live oak	102	--	--	102
Oregon white oak	502	--	--	502
California black oak	555	--	98	652
Hardwood total	4,417	580	181	5,178
All species	16,701	4,988	3,323	25,012

Data Table NC-DF 1 -- Area of Non-coastal Douglas-fir forest by trees-per-acre class and State, BLM land, 2005.

Trees/acre	State							All states
	CO	ID	MT	OR	UT	WA	WY	
	- - - - - - - - Thousand acres - - - - - - - -							
< 100	92	91	85	2	23	--	2	295
100 - 199	15	83	136	--	13	18	5	269
200 - 299	29	69	--	--	24	18	6	146
300 - 399	4	--	61	--	--	13	17	94
400 - 499	15	24	21	12	5	--	14	91
500 - 599	38	--	20	--	2	--	--	60
600 - 699	--	--	--	--	--	--	--	--
700 - 799	--	--	--	--	8	--	6	15
800 - 899	17	--	40	--	--	--	--	58
900 - 999	34	--	18	--	--	--	6	58
1000 +	--	--	55	--	7	--	9	71
All classes	244	267	436	14	82	49	65	1,156

Data Table NC-DF 2 -- Area of Non-coastal Douglas-fir forest by State and stand-size class, BLM land, 2005.

State	Stand-size class				
	Sparse stands (<10% stocked)	Seedlings/saplings (0-4.9" dbh/drc)	Medium trees (5-9" or 5-11" dbh/drc)	Large trees (9 or 11"+ dbh/drc)	Total
	- - - - - - - - - - Thousand acres - - - - - - - - - -				
Colorado	17	15	13	197	244
Idaho	8	--	25	234	267
Montana	12	37	80	307	436
Oregon	--	--	12	2	14
Utah	--	20	11	52	82
Washington	--	--	--	49	49
Wyoming	--	--	14	51	65
All states	37	72	155	892	1,156

Data Table NC-DF 3 -- Area of Non-coastal Douglas-fir forest by stand-age class and State, BLM land, 2005.

Stand-age class	State							All states
	CO	ID	MT	OR	UT	WA	WY	
	- - - - - - - - Thousand acres - - - - - - - -							
Unavailable	17	8	12	--	--	--	--	37
1 - 50 years	15	--	37	12	20	--	--	84
51 - 100 years	91	171	210	2	19	36	16	545
101 - 150 years	68	57	101	--	31	13	27	296
151 - 200 years	31	32	54	--	--	--	6	122
201 - 250 years	20	--	16	--	13	--	17	67
251 - 300 years	--	--	5	--	--	--	--	5
Grand Total	244	267	436	14	82	49	65	1,156

Data Table NC-DF 4 -- Area of Non-coastal Douglas-fir forest by live-tree basal area class and State, BLM land, 2005.

Basal area class (ft^2/acre)	State							All states
	CO	ID	MT	OR	UT	WA	WY	
	- - - - - - - - Thousand acres - - - - - - - -							
0 - 25	17	8	12	2	--	--	1	40
26 - 50	62	25	21	--	18	--	1	127
51 - 75	43	52	171	--	16	--	19	302
76 - 100	27	89	72	12	18	--	13	230
101 - 125	--	69	--	--	7	18	--	95
126 - 150	67	24	39	--	24	18	17	189
151 - 175	13	--	65	--	--	13	--	91
176 - 200	13	--	14	--	--	--	9	36
201 - 225	--	--	26	--	--	--	--	26
226 - 250	--	--	16	--	--	--	6	22
All classes	244	267	436	14	82	49	65	1,156

Data Table NC-DF 5 -- Area of Non-coastal Douglas-fir forest by State and percent stand density index (SDI), BLM land, 2005.

State	Percent of maximum SDI				Total
	< 25	25.0 - 34.9	35.0 - 59.9	60 +	
	- - - - - - - - - - Thousand acres - - - - - - - - - -				
Colorado	104	47	67	26	244
Idaho	85	89	93	--	267
Montana	161	79	88	108	436
Oregon	2	--	12	--	14
Utah	21	28	26	7	82
Washington	--	18	31	--	49
Wyoming	7	27	9	23	65
All states	379	288	325	165	1,156

Data Table NC-DF 6 -- Number of standing dead trees on Non-coastal Douglas-fir forests by species and diameter class, BLM land, 2005.

Species	Diameter class (inches)			All classes
	5.0-10.9	11.0-18.9	19.0+	
	- - - - - - - - - Thousand trees - - - - - - - - -			
Pacific silver fir	228	152	--	380
White fir	186	--	--	186
Utah juniper	76	105	--	181
Rocky Mountain juniper	333	93	--	426
Western larch	--	109	--	109
Engelmann spruce	86	--	--	86
Common pinyon	746	93	--	839
Lodgepole pine	578	161	--	740
Limber pine	3,277	671	--	3,948
Western white pine	76	76	--	152
Ponderosa pine	132	241	87	460
Douglas-fir	7,273	2,539	697	10,509
Softwood total	12,992	4,240	784	18,016
Curlleaf mountain-mahogany	1,149	--	--	1,149
Quaking aspen	1,086	143	--	1,229
Hardwood total	2,234	143	--	2,378
All species	15,226	4,383	784	20,393

Data Table WJ 1 -- Area of Western juniper forest by trees-per-acre class and State, BLM land, 2005.

Trees/acre	State				All states
	CA	ID	NV	OR	
	- - - - - - - - - Thousand acres - - - - - - - - -				
< 100	200	145	55	1,208	1,609
100 - 199	66	24	--	127	216
200 - 299	--	24	--	43	66
300 - 399	12	24	--	14	49
400 +	--	--	--	7	7
All classes	278	217	55	1,398	1,948

Data Table WJ 2 -- Area of Western juniper forest by State and stand-size class, BLM land, 2005.

State	Stand-size class				
	Sparse stands (<10% stocked)	Seedlings/saplings (0-4.9" dbh/drc)	Medium trees (5-9" or 5-11" dbh/drc)	Large trees (9 or 11"+ dbh/drc)	Total
	- - - - - - - - - - Thousand acres - - - - - - - - - -				
California	23	32	28	195	278
Idaho	68	48	--	101	217
Nevada	55	--	--	--	55
Oregon	441	186	13	758	1,398
All states	588	265	41	1,054	1,948

Data Table WJ 3 -- Area of Western juniper forest by stand-age class and State, BLM land, 2005.

Stand-age class	State				All states
	CA	ID	NV	OR	
	- - - - - - - - - - Thousand acres - - - - - - -				
Unavailable	35	68	55	441	599
1 - 50 years	64	48	--	48	159
51 - 100 years	146	24	--	542	712
101 - 150 years	33	24	--	84	141
151 - 200 years	--	54	--	156	209
201 - 250 years	--	--	--	84	84
251 - 300 years	--	--	--	43	43
All classes	278	217	55	1,398	1,948

Data Table WJ 4 -- Area of Western juniper forest by live-tree basal area class and State, BLM land, 2005.

State

Basal area class (ft²/acre)	CA	ID	NV	OR	All states
	- - - - - - - - - Thousand acres - - - - - - - - -				
0 - 25	97	116	55	715	984
26 - 50	132	24	--	410	565
51 - 75	27	48	--	176	251
76 - 100	22	30	--	50	101
101 +	--	--	--	47	47
All classes	278	217	55	1,398	1,948

Data Table WJ 5 -- Area of Western juniper forest by State and percent stand density index (SDI), BLM land, 2005.

State	Percent of maximum SDI				Total
	< 25	25.0 - 34.9	35.0 - 59.9	60 +	
	- - - - - - - - - - Thousand acres - - - - - - - - - -				
California	222	19	37	--	278
Idaho	116	72	30	--	217
Nevada	55	--	--	--	55
Oregon	1,140	148	77	33	1,398
All states	1,533	238	144	33	1,948

Data Table WJ 6 -- Number of standing dead trees on Western juniper forests by species and diameter class, BLM land, 2005.

Species	Diameter class (inches)			All classes
	5.0-10.9	11.0-18.9	19.0+	
	- - - - - - - - - Thousand trees - - - - - - - - -			
Western juniper	2,393	1,002	539	3,935
Softwood total	2,393	1,002	539	3,935
Curlleaf mountain-mahogany	723	156	--	879
Chokecherry	98	--	--	98
Hardwood total	821	156	--	977
All species	3,214	1,158	539	4,912

Data Table PP 1 -- Area of ponderosa pine forest by trees-per-acre class and State, BLM land, 2005.

State		All

Trees/acre	AZ	CO	MT	NM	OR	SD	UT	WY	states
	- - - - - - - - - Thousand acres - - - - - - - -								
< 100	--	85	190	28	25	--	10	36	373
100 - 199	--	25	40	5	85	12	28	24	219
200 - 299	--	15	105	13	9	--	10	7	159
300 - 399	13	--	30	--	47	--	3	10	103
400 - 499	--	--	35	7	--	--	--	7	48
500 - 599	--	--	--	--	2	--	--	--	2
600 - 699	--	--	--	--	--	--	--	6	6
700 - 799	--	18	34	--	--	--	--	--	52
800 - 899	--	--	--	--	32	--	--	6	38
900 - 999	--	--	--	5	--	--	--	--	5
1000 +	--	15	20	5	27	--	--	--	67
All classes	13	159	454	62	226	12	51	95	1,072

Data Table PP 2 -- Area of ponderosa pine forest by State and stand-size class, BLM land, 2005.

State	Stand-size class				
	Sparse stands (<10% stocked)	Seedlings/saplings (0-4.9" dbh/drc)	Medium trees (5-9" or 5-11" dbh/drc)	Large trees (9 or 11"+ dbh/drc)	Total
	- - - - - - - - - - Thousand acres - - - - - - - - - -				
Arizona	--	--	--	13	13
Colorado	39	16	--	104	159
Montana	113	26	35	280	454
New Mexico	14	--	5	42	62
Oregon	20	3	--	204	226
South Dakota	--	--	--	12	12
Utah	10	--	--	41	51
Wyoming	21	--	11	63	95
All states	218	44	51	759	1,072

Data Table PP 3 -- Area of ponderosa pine forest by stand-age class and State, BLM land, 2005.

Stand-age class	State								All States
	AZ	CO	MT	NM	OR	SD	UT	WY	
	- - - - - - - Thousand acres - - - - - - -								

	AZ	CO	MT	NM	OR	SD	UT	WY	Grand Total
Unavailable	--	39	113	14	20	--	10	21	218
1 - 50 years	--	16	26	--	29	12	--	--	82
51 - 100 years	--	33	188	36	155	--	3	31	446
101 - 150 years	13	71	122	--	22	--	--	34	261
151 - 200 years	--	--	5	12	--	--	10	9	36
201 - 250 years	--	--	--	--	--	--	28	--	28
Grand Total	13	159	454	62	226	12	51	95	1,072

Data Table PP 4 -- Area of ponderosa pine forest by live-tree basal area class and State, BLM land, 2005.

Basal area class (ft²/acre)	State								All States
	AZ	CO	MT	NM	OR	SD	UT	WY	
- - - - - - - Thousand acres - - - - - -									
0 - 25	--	55	144	14	25	--	10	28	276
26 - 50	--	42	113	13	18	--	24	10	221
51 - 75	--	46	123	10	32	12	10	25	258
76 - 100	--	--	--	10	23	--	--	10	42
101 - 125	13	--	54	7	22	--	--	6	101
126 - 150	--	--	--	7	30	--	7	13	57
151 - 175	--	15	--	--	12	--	--	--	28
176 - 200	--	--	20	--	12	--	--	6	38
201 +	--	--	--	--	51	--	--	--	51
All classes	13	159	454	62	226	12	51	95	1,072

Data Table PP 5 -- Area of ponderosa pine forest by State and percent stand density index (SDI), BLM land, 2005.

State	Percent of maximum SDI				Total
	< 25	25.0 - 34.9	35.0 - 59.9	60 +	
- - - - - - - - - - Thousand acres - - - - - - - - - -					

Arizona	--	--	13	--	13
Colorado	97	46	--	15	159
Montana	278	66	55	56	454
New Mexico	28	10	24	--	62
Oregon	59	16	75	76	226
South Dakota	--	12	--	--	12
Utah	34	10	7	--	51
Wyoming	44	17	11	24	95
All states	540	177	185	171	1,072

Data Table PP 6 -- Number of standing dead trees on ponderosa pine forests by species and diameter class, BLM land, 2005.

	Diameter class (inches)			All
Species	5.0- 10.9	11.0- 18.9	19.0+	classes
	- - - - - - - - Thousand trees - - - - - - - -			
White fir	166	--	--	166
Rocky Mountain juniper	886	143	--	1,030
Oneseed juniper	--	43	--	43
Incense-cedar	575	--	16	592
Bristlecone pine	81	--	--	81
Knobcone pine	83	83	--	166
Limber pine	34	--	--	34
Sugar pine	--	--	22	22
Ponderosa pine	4,587	608	10	5,205
Singleleaf pinyon	57	--	--	57
Douglas-fir	1,871	400	22	2,293
Softwood total	8,340	1,278	70	9,688
Pacific madrone	412	--	--	412
Curlleaf mountain-mahogany	99	58	--	158
California black oak	133	--	--	133
Hardwood total	644	58	--	703
All species	8,984	1,336	70	10,390

Data Table DOW 1 -- Area of deciduous oak woodland by trees-per-acre class and State, BLM land, 2005.

	State						All
Trees/acre	AZ	CA	CO	NV	NM	UT	states
	- - - - - - - - Thousand acres - - - - - - - -						

	AZ	CA	CO	NV	NM	UT	All states
< 100	10	8	67	30	7	78	200
100 - 199	--	--	88	--	--	1	89
200 - 299	--	--	15	--	--	--	15
300 - 399	--	--	17	--	--	19	36
400 - 499	--	--	57	--	--	26	83
500 - 599	--	--	28	22	--	17	67
600 - 699	--	--	68	--	--	--	68
700 - 799	--	--	12	--	--	10	22
800 - 899	--	--	--	--	--	--	--
900 - 999	--	--	--	--	6	19	24
1000 - 1999	--	--	68	22	--	57	147
2000 - 2999	--	--	47	--	2	30	79
3000 - 3999	--	--	69	--	--	35	104
4000 +	--	--	22	--	--	9	32
All classes	10	8	558	75	15	300	965

Data Table DOW 2 -- Area of deciduous oak woodland by State and stand-size class, BLM land, 2005.

	Stand-size class				
State	Sparse stands (<10% stocked)	Seedlings/saplings (0-4.9" dbh/drc)	Medium trees (5-9" or 5-11" dbh/drc)	Large trees (9 or 11"+ dbh/drc)	Total
	- - - - - - - - - - Thousand acres - - - - - - - - - -				
Arizona	--	10	--	--	10
California	--	--	--	8	8
Colorado	49	505	4	--	558
Nevada	--	75	--	--	75
New Mexico	--	9	--	6	15
Utah	11	284	1	4	300
All states	60	883	4	18	965

Data Table DOW 3 -- Area of deciduous oak woodland by stand-age class and State, BLM land, 2005.

	State						All
Stand-age class	AZ	CA	CO	NV	NM	UT	states
	- - - - - - - - - Thousand acres - - - - - - - - -						
Unavailable	--	8	49	--	--	11	68
1 - 25 years	10	--	396	7	75	227	714

26 - 50 years	--	--	89	2	--	52	143
51 - 75 years	--	--	24	--	--	6	30
76 - 100 years	--	--	--	--	--	4	4
101 - 125 years	--	--	--	6	--	--	6
All classes	10	8	558	15	75	300	965

Data Table DOW 4 -- Area of deciduous oak woodland by live-tree basal area class and State, BLM land, 2005.

Basal area class (ft²/acre)	State						All states
	AZ	CA	CO	NV	NM	UT	
	- - - - - - - - *Thousand acres* - - - - - - - -						
0 - 25	10	8	262	52	7	133	472
26 - 50	--	--	174	22	--	89	286
51 - 75	--	--	63	--	--	54	118
76 - 100	--	--	33	--	6	9	48
101 +	--	--	25	--	2	14	41
All classes	10	8	558	75	15	300	965

Data Table DOW 5 -- Area of deciduous oak woodland by State and percent stand density index (SDI), BLM land, 2005.

| State | Percent of maximum SDI | | | | Total |
	< 25	25.0 - 34.9	35.0 - 59.9	60 +	
	- - - - - - - - - - Thousand acres - - - - - - - - - -				
Arizona	10	--	--	--	10
California	8	--	--	--	8
Colorado	391	70	68	29	558
Nevada	75	--	--	--	75
New Mexico	7	--	6	2	15
Utah	192	45	40	23	300
All states	682	115	114	54	965

Data Table DOW 6 -- Number of standing dead trees on deciduous oak woodlands by species and diameter class, BLM land, 2005.

| Species | Diameter class (inches) | | | All classes |
	5.0- 10.9	11.0- 18.9	19.0+	
	- - - - - - - - - Thousand trees - - - - - - - - -			
Utah juniper	813	323	--	1,136
Rocky Mountain juniper	93	--	--	93
Common pinyon	1,047	282	--	1,329
Ponderosa pine	89	212	56	357
Singleleaf pinyon	721	--	--	721
Douglas-fir	1,107	501	145	1,753
Softwood total	3,869	1,319	201	5,389
Quaking aspen	95	--	--	95
Gambel oak	1,275	--	--	1,275
Hardwood total	1,370	--	--	1,370
All species	5,240	1,319	201	6,759

Data Table CW 1 -- Area of *Cercocarpus* woodland by trees-per-acre class and State, BLM land, 2005.

Trees/acre	State								All States
	CA	CO	ID	MT	NV	OR	UT	WY	
	------- *Thousand acres* --------								
< 100	12	--	--	--	93	30	10	10	154
100 - 199	40	--	18	--	31	--	22	--	113
200 - 299	15	--	--	--	73	--	20	--	108
300 - 399	--	16	33	21	21	--	8	9	108
400 - 499	--	--	--	--	13	--	29	--	42
500 - 599	--	--	--	--	--	--	--	--	--
600 - 699	--	--	--	--	--	--	27	--	27
700 - 799	--	--	--	--	--	--	--	--	--
800 - 899	--	--	--	--	--	--	20	6	26
900 - 999	--	--	--	--	26	--	--	--	26
1000 +	--	4	--	17	8	--	10	--	38
All classes	67	20	52	37	265	30	146	25	642

Data Table CW 2 -- Area of *Cercocarpus* woodland by State and stand-size class, BLM land, 2005.

State	Stand-size class				Total
	Sparse stands (<10% stocked)	Seedlings/saplings (0-4.9" dbh/drc)	Medium trees (5-9" or 5-11" dbh/drc)	Large trees (9 or 11"+ dbh/drc)	
	---------- *Thousand acres* ----------				
California	--	--	15	52	67
Colorado	--	--	4	16	20
Idaho	--	--	33	18	52
Montana	--	37	--	--	37
Nevada	29	37	21	178	265
Oregon	--	14	--	16	30
Utah	10	9	30	96	146
Wyoming	10	6	--	9	25
All states	49	103	104	386	642

Data Table CW 3 -- Area of *Cercocarpus* woodland by stand-age class and State, BLM land, 2005.

Stand-age class	State								All states
	CA	CO	ID	MT	NV	OR	UT	WY	
	— — — — — — — — — *Thousand acres* — — — — — — — — —								
Unavailable	12	--	--	--	29	--	10	10	61
1 - 25 years	--	--	--	--	--	14	9	6	29
26 - 50 years	15	--	--	21	29	--	--	9	73
51 - 75 years	--	--	--	17	8	--	9	--	34
76 - 100 years	15	4	33	--	21	16	31	--	121
101 - 125 years	12	--	--	--	64	--	29	--	105
126 - 150 years	--	16	18	--	83	--	36	--	154
151 - 175 years	--	--	--	--	31	--	13	--	44
176 - 200 years	14	--	--	--	--	--	8	--	22
Grand Total	67	20	52	37	265	30	146	25	642

Data Table CW 4 -- Area of *Cercocarpus* woodland by basal area class and State, BLM land, 2005.

Basal area class (ft^2/acre)	State								All States
	CA	CO	ID	MT	NV	OR	UT	WY	
	— — — — — — — — *Thousand acres* — — — — — —								
0 - 25	--	--	--	21	101	14	10	10	156
26 - 50	--	--	18	--	52	16	28	6	121
51 - 75	12	16	33	--	--	--	40	--	102
76 - 100	42	4	--	--	43	--	7	9	104
101 - 125	--	--	--	17	28	--	38	--	83
126 - 150	--	--	--	--	--	--	4	--	4
151 - 175	14	--	--	--	8	--	10	--	31
176 - 200	--	--	--	--	26	--	--	--	26
201 +	--	--	--	--	8	--	8	--	16
All classes	67	20	52	37	265	30	146	25	642

Data Table CW 5 -- Area of *Cercocarpus* woodland by State and percent stand density index (SDI), BLM land, 2005.

State	Percent of maximum SDI				Total
	< 25	25.0 - 34.9	35.0 - 59.9	60 +	
	- - - - - - - - - - - Thousand acres - - - - - - - - - - -				
California	--	12	42	14	67
Colorado	--	16	4	--	20
Idaho	18	33	--	--	52
Montana	21	--	--	17	37
Nevada	153	--	70	41	265
Oregon	30	--	--	--	30
Utah	38	40	40	28	146
Wyoming	10	6	9	--	25
All states	270	108	164	100	642

Data Table CW 6 -- Number of standing dead trees on *Cercocarpus* woodlands by species and diameter class, BLM land, 2005.

Species	Diameter class (inches)			All classes
	5.0-10.9	11.0-18.9	19.0+	
	- - - - - - - - - Thousand trees - - - - - - - - -			
White fir	57	--	--	57
Western juniper	140	--	70	210
Utah juniper	61	--	--	61
Common pinyon	116	116	--	232
Limber pine	--	--	124	124
Singleleaf pinyon	--	57	191	248
Softwood total	375	173	385	933
Curlleaf mountain-mahogany	9,468	2,022	57	11,546
Quaking aspen	232	58	--	290
Gambel oak	95	--	--	95
Hardwood total	9,796	2,080	57	11,932
All species	10,170	2,252	442	12,865

Data Table AS 1 -- Area of aspen forest by trees-per-acre class and State, BLM land, 2005.

Trees/acre	State CO	ID	NV	OR	UT	WY	All states
	- - - - - - - - - Thousand acres - - - - - - - - -						
< 100	32	--	--	24	9	16	82
100 - 199	3	--	31	--	--	10	43
200 - 299	26	--	--	--	--	5	31
300 - 399	37	--	--	--	--	16	54
400 - 499	50	37	--	--	2	6	95
500 - 599	11	--	--	--	--	4	14
600 - 699	--	--	--	--	--	4	4
700 - 799	17	--	--	--	--	--	17
800 - 899	--	--	--	--	--	--	--
900 - 999	10	--	--	--	--	5	14
1000 +	--	--	--	2	--	11	13
All classes	187	37	31	26	11	77	368

Data Table AS 2 -- Area of aspen forest by State and stand-size class, BLM land, 2005.

State	Stand-size class Sparse stands (<10% stocked)	Seedlings/saplings (0-4.9" dbh/drc)	Medium trees (5-9" or 5-11" dbh/drc)	Large trees (9 or 11"+ dbh/drc)	Total
	- - - - - - - - - - Thousand acres - - - - - - - - - -				
Colorado	13	25	132	17	187
Idaho	--	--	--	37	37
Nevada	--	--	31	--	31
Oregon	--	16	9	--	26
Utah	--	9	--	2	11
Wyoming	--	30	41	6	77
All states	13	81	213	61	368

Data Table AS 3 -- Area of aspen forest by stand-age class and State, BLM land, 2005.

Stand-age class	State						All States
	CO	ID	NV	OR	UT	WY	
	- - - -- - - - - Thousand acres - - - - - - -						
Unavailable	13	--	--	--	--	--	13
1 - 25 years	--	--	--	16	9	24	49
26 - 50 years	15	--	--	--	--	6	22
51 - 75 years	63	--	--	--	--	17	80
76 - 100 years	89	37	31	8	--	19	183
101 - 125 years	3	--	--	--	--	9	12
126 - 150 years	4	--	--	--	--	1	5
151 - 175 years	--	--	--	--	2	--	2
176 - 200 years	--	--	--	2	--	--	2
All classes	187	37	31	26	11	77	368

Data Table AS 4 -- Area of aspen forest by live-tree basal area class and State, BLM land, 2005.

Basal area class (ft²/acre)	State						All States
	CO	ID	NV	OR	UT	WY	
	- - - - - - - - Thousand acres - - - - - - - -						
0 - 25	28	--	31	16	9	27	111
26 - 50	35	--	--	--	--	13	48
51 - 75	18	37	--	8	--	6	68
76 - 100	38	--	--	--	--	15	54
101 - 125	--	--	--	--	--	--	--
126 - 150	32	--	--	2	2	11	46
151 - 175	18	--	--	--	--	--	18
176 - 200	--	--	--	--	--	4	4
201 +	17	--	--	--	--	1	18
All classes	187	37	31	26	11	77	368

Data Table AS 5 -- Area of aspen forest by State and percent stand density index (SDI), BLM land, 2005.

State	Percent of maximum SDI					Total
	< 25	25.0 - 34.9	35.0 - 59.9		60 +	
		- - - - - - - - - - Thousand acres - - - - - - - - - -				
Colorado	81	20		50	35	187
Idaho	--	37		--	--	37
Nevada	31	--		--	--	31
Oregon	24	--		--	2	26
Utah	9	--		2	--	11
Wyoming	42	16		9	11	77
All states	187	72		61	48	368

Data Table AS 6 -- Number of standing dead trees on aspen forests by species and diameter class, BLM land, 2005.

Species	Diameter class (inches)			All classes
	5.0-10.9	11.0-18.9	19.0+	
	- - - - - - - - - Thousand trees - - - - - - - - -			
White fir	850	397	--	1,246
Subalpine fir	1,366	105	--	1,471
Engelmann spruce	52	52	--	103
Bristlecone pine	123	--	--	123
Lodgepole pine	413	52	--	464
Limber pine	103	--	--	103
Douglas-fir	175	--	57	231
Softwood total	3,082	605	57	3,743
Quaking aspen	7,158	233	--	7,391
Hardwood total	7,158	233	--	7,391
All species	10,239	838	57	11,134

Data Table LP 1 -- Area of lodgepole pine forest by trees-per-acre class and State, BLM land, 2005.

Trees/acre	CO	MT	OR	WY	All states
	\-\-\-\-\-\-\-\-\- Thousand acres \-\-\-\-\-\-\-\-\-				
< 100	--	6	41	8	55
100 - 199	5	--	--	--	5
200 - 299	--	24	--	31	55
300 - 399	--	40	--	5	45
400 - 499	45	--	30	9	83
500 - 599	--	20	--	6	26
600 - 699	--	19	--	6	25
700 - 799	15	--	--	13	28
800 - 899	15	--	--	--	15
900 - 999	--	--	--	--	--
1000 +	15	--	--	9	24
All classes	94	110	71	85	359

Data Table LP 2 -- Area of lodgepole pine forest by State and stand-size class, BLM land, 2005.

State	Sparse stands (<10% stocked)	Seedlings/saplings (0-4.9" dbh/drc)	Medium trees (5-9" or 5-11" dbh/drc)	Large trees (9 or 11"+ dbh/drc)	Total
	\-\-\-\-\-\-\-\-\-\- Thousand acres \-\-\-\-\-\-\-\-\-\-				
Colorado	--	--	64	30	94
Montana	--	6	39	64	110
Oregon	--	61	10	--	71
Wyoming	8	11	39	28	85
All states	8	77	153	122	359

Data Table LP 3 -- Area of lodgepole pine forest by stand-age class and State, BLM land, 2005.

Stand-age class	CO	MT	OR	WY	All states
	\-\-\-\-\-\-\-\-\- Thousand acres \-\-\-\-\-\-\-\-\-				
Unavailable	--	--	--	8	8
1 - 25 years	--	6	41	5	52
26 - 50 years	--	--	16	6	22
51 - 75 years	--	19	13	21	54
76 - 100 years	42	--	--	27	69
101 - 125 years	48	64	--	14	126
126 - 150 years	5	--	--	4	9
151 - 175 years	--	20	--	--	20
All classes	94	110	71	85	359

Data Table LP 4 -- Area of lodgepole pine forest by live-tree basal area class and State, BLM land, 2005.

| Basal area class | State | | | | All |
(ft²/acre)	CO	MT	OR	WY	states
	- - - - - - - - - Thousand acres - - - - - - - - -				
0 - 25	--	6	31	8	45
26 - 50	5	--	24	--	28
51 - 75	--	--	16	11	28
76 - 100	30	--	--	19	49
101 - 125	--	45	--	27	72
126 - 150	30	19	--	6	54
151 - 175	15	20	--	7	42
176 - 200	15	20	--	6	40
201+	--	--	--	2	2
All classes	94	110	71	85	359

Data Table LP 5 -- Area of lodgepole pine forest by State and percent stand density index (SDI), BLM land, 2005.

| | Percent of maximum SDI | | | | |
State	< 25	25.0 - 34.9	35.0 - 59.9	60 +	Total
	- - - - - - - - - - - - Thousand acres - - - - - - - - - -				
Colorado	5	--	74	15	94
Montana	6	--	84	20	110
Oregon	71	--	--	--	71
Wyoming	19	13	39	15	85
All states	100	13	197	49	359

Data Table LP 6 -- Number of standing dead trees on lodgepole pine forests by species and diameter class, BLM land, 2005.

| | Diameter class (inches) | | | All |
Species	5.0-10.9	11.0-18.9	19.0+	classes
	- - - - - - - - - - Thousand trees - - - - - - - - - -			
Subalpine fir	723	--	--	723
Lodgepole pine	9,638	178	35	9,851
Limber pine	68	--	--	68
Douglas-fir	617	269	52	937
Softwood total	11,045	447	86	11,578
Quaking aspen	245	--	--	245
Hardwood total	245	--	--	245
All species	11,290	447	86	11,823

Data Table AZ 1 -- Area of forest land by forest type and stand-size class, Arizona BLM land, 2005.

Forest type	Stand-size class				
	Sparse stands (<10% stocked)	Seedlings/ saplings (0-4.9" dbh/drc)	Medium trees (5-9" or 5-11" dbh/drc)	Large trees (9 or 11"+ dbh/drc)	Total
	- - - - - - - - - Thousand acres - - - - - - - - -				
Juniper woodland	125	12	--	383	520
Pinyon / juniper woodland	137	90	37	751	1,015
Ponderosa pine	--	--	--	13	13
Deciduous oak woodland	--	10	--	--	10
Evergreen oak woodland	--	--	--	23	23
Mesquite woodland	151	48	11	85	296
Misc. western hardwood woodland	--	17	--	--	17
All types	413	176	48	1,255	1,893

Data Table AZ 2 -- Gross annual growth, annual mortality, and net annual growth of all trees on forest land by species, Arizona BLM land, 2005.

Species	Gross annual growth	Annual mortality	Net annual growth
	- - - - - - - Thousand cubic feet - - - - - - -		
Redberry juniper	9	80	-72
California juniper	80	62	18
Alligator juniper	26	--	26
Utah juniper	2,913	768	2,145
Oneseed juniper	316	--	316
Common or twoneedle pinyon	1,021	931	90
Ponderosa pine	370	--	370
Singleleaf pinyon	797	69	728
Border pinyon	11	--	11
Mexican pinyon pine	63	--	63
Arizona pinyon pine	13	--	13
Softwood total	5,618	1,911	3,708
Fremont cottonwood,Rio Grande cottonwood	3	--	3
Western honey mesquite	1	--	1
Velvet mesquite	204	--	204
Arizona white oak/gray oak	52	--	52
Emory oak	2	5	-3
Gambel oak	6	--	6
Silverleaf oak	16	--	16
Hardwood total	285	5	280
All species	5,903	1,916	3,988

Data Table CA 1 -- Area of forest land by forest type and stand-size class, California BLM land, 2005.

Forest type	Stand-size class				
	Sparse stands (<10% stocked)	Seedlings/saplings (0-4.9" dbh/drc)	Medium trees (5-9" or 5-11" dbh/drc)	Large trees (9 or 11"+ dbh/drc)	Total
	- - - - - - - - - - Thousand acres - - - - - - - - - -				
Western Juniper	23	32	28	195	278
Juniper woodland	77	14	--	46	137
Pinyon / juniper woodland	94	48	14	148	303
Douglas-fir	--	--	--	17	17
Misc. western softwoods	14	--	--	3	17
California mixed conifer	--	--	--	74	74
Cottonwood / willow	--	--	--	11	11
Oregon ash	--	--	1	--	1
Gray pine	17	--	4	--	21
California black oak	--	--	7	17	24
Oregon white oak	--	27	1	17	45
Blue oak	37	17	--	36	90
Deciduous oak woodland	--	--	--	8	8
Canyon live oak / interior live oak	19	82	45	86	232
Tanoak	--	5	24	21	49
Mesquite woodland	16	--	--	11	27
Cercocarpus woodland	--	--	15	52	67
Misc. western hardwood woodland	15	--	--	--	15
Nonstocked	20	12	--	--	31
All types	333	236	139	741	1,449

Data Table CO 1 -- Area of forest land by forest type and stand-size class, Colorado BLM land, 2005.

Forest type	Sparse stands (<10% stocked)	Seedlings/saplings (0-4.9" dbh/drc)	Medium trees (5-9" or 5-11" dbh/drc)	Large trees (9 or 11"+ dbh/drc)	Total
			Stand-size class		
	--------- Thousand acres ---------				
Rocky Mountain juniper	--	--	--	185	185
Juniper woodland	52	12	--	589	653
Pinyon / juniper woodland	232	141	32	2,447	2,852
Douglas-fir	17	15	13	197	244
Ponderosa pine	39	16	--	104	159
Engelmann spruce	--	--	15	51	66
Subalpine fir	--	--	6	35	41
Lodgepole pine	--	--	64	30	94
Limber pine	--	--	--	3	3
Cottonwood	10	--	--	4	15
Aspen	13	25	132	17	187
Deciduous oak woodland	49	505	4	--	558
Cercocarpus woodland	--	--	4	16	20
All types	413	714	270	3,679	5,076

Data Table CO 2 -- Gross annual growth, annual mortality, and net annual growth of all trees on forest land by species, Colorado BLM land, 2005.

Species	Gross annual growth	Annual mortality	Net annual growth
	- - - - - - - - - Thousand cubic feet - - - - - - -		
White fir	144	--	144
Subalpine fir	2,915	3,879	-964
Utah juniper	7,669	1,101	6,568
Rocky Mountain juniper	994	95	898
Oneseed juniper	145	--	145
Engelmann spruce	3,468	19	3,450
Blue spruce	158	--	158
Rocky Mountain bristlecone pine	432	272	161
Common or twoneedle pinyon	10,689	9,617	1,073
Lodgepole pine	5,596	1,205	4,391
Limber pine	217	--	217
Ponderosa pine	2,112	--	2,112
Douglas-fir	7,983	1,423	6,561
Softwood total	42,524	17,609	24,915
Curlleaf mountain-mahogany	98	--	98
Aspen	4,588	1,231	3,358
Fremont cottonwood,Rio Grande cottonwood	29	233	-204
Narrowleaf cottonwood	27	--	27
Gambel oak	651	145	506
Hardwood total	5,393	1,608	3,784
All species	47,917	19,218	28,699

Data Table ID 1 -- Area of forest land by forest type and stand-size class, Idaho BLM land, 2005.

Forest type	Stand-size class				
	Sparse stands (<10% stocked)	Seedlings/saplings (0-4.9" dbh/drc)	Medium trees (5-9" or 5-11" dbh/drc)	Large trees (9 or 11"+ dbh/drc)	Total
	- - - - - - - - - - Thousand acres - - - - - - - - - -				
Rocky Mountain juniper	--	--	--	42	42
Western Juniper	68	48	--	101	217
Juniper woodland	36	--	--	103	140
Pinyon / juniper woodland	--	--	--	29	29
Douglas-fir	8	--	25	234	267
Grand fir	--	--	--	63	63
Subalpine fir	--	--	--	29	29
Whitebark pine	--	--	--	15	15
Cottonwood	--	--	--	26	26
Aspen	--	--	--	37	37
Paper birch	--	--	29	--	29
Cercocarpus woodland	--	--	33	18	52
All types	112	48	87	698	945

Data Table ID 2 -- Gross annual growth, annual mortality, and net annual growth of all trees on forest land by species, Idaho BLM land, 2005.

Species	Gross annual growth	Annual mortality	Net annual growth
	- - - - - - - - Thousand cubic feet - - - - - - - -		
Grand fir	6,686	--	6,686
Subalpine fir	1,005	--	1,005
Western juniper	1,152	--	1,152
Utah juniper	734	1,082	-348
Rocky Mountain juniper	143	--	143
Western larch	89	--	89
Whitebark pine	165	--	165
Western white pine	294	--	294
Ponderosa pine	641	--	641
Singleleaf pinyon	121	--	121
Douglas-fir	10,180	2,546	7,634
Western redcedar	1,080	--	1,080
Western hemlock	108	--	108
Softwood total	22,398	3,627	18,771
Paper birch	1,028	--	1,028
Curlleaf mountain-mahogany	160	--	160
Aspen	2,191	--	2,191
Black cottonwood	1,836	--	1,836
Hardwood total	5,215	--	5,215
All species	27,613	3,627	23,986

Data Table MT 1 -- Area of forest land by forest type and stand-size class, Montana, North Dakota, and South Dakota BLM land, 2005.

Forest type	Sparse stands (<10% stocked)	Seedlings/ saplings (0-4.9" dbh/ drc)	Medium trees (5-9" or 5-11" dbh/drc)	Large trees (9 or 11"+ dbh/drc)	Total
	--------- Thousand acres ---------				
White spruce	--	--	7	--	7
Rocky Mountain juniper	36	43	5	72	156
Juniper woodland	--	--	--	35	35
Douglas-fir	12	37	80	307	436
Ponderosa pine	113	26	35	292	466
Engelmann spruce	--	--	--	4	4
Engelman spruce / subalpine fir	6	--	33	--	39
Lodgepole pine	--	6	39	64	110
Limber pine	20	--	--	--	20
Bur oak	--	--	6	--	6
Mixed upland hardwood	--	--	7	--	7
Sugarberry / hackberry / elm / green ash	--	1	--	--	1
Cercocarpus woodland	--	37	--	--	37
All types	187	150	213	774	1,326

Data Table MT 2 -- Gross annual growth, annual mortality, and net annual growth of all trees on forest land by species, Montana BLM land, 2005.

Species	Gross annual growth	Annual mortality	Net annual growth
	-------- Thousand cubic feet --------		
Subalpine fir	3,699	292	3,407
Utah juniper	89	--	89
Rocky Mountain juniper	941	192	749
Western larch	717	--	717
Engelmann spruce	3,660	--	3,660
Whitebark pine	83	--	83
Lodgepole pine	6,684	4,983	1,702
Limber pine	369	1,238	-869
Ponderosa pine	6,580	4,268	2,312
Douglas-fir	13,229	173	13,056
Softwood total	36,050	11,146	24,904
Curlleaf mountain-mahogany	27	--	27
Aspen	9	--	9
Hardwood total	36	--	36
All species	36,086	11,146	24,940

Data Table NV 1 -- Area of forest land by forest type and stand-size class, Nevada BLM land, 2005.

Forest type	Sparse stands (<10% stocked)	Seedlings/saplings (0-4.9" dbh/drc)	Medium trees (5-9" or 5-11" dbh/drc)	Large trees (9 or 11"+ dbh/drc)	Total
			Stand-size class		
	---------- Thousand acres ----------				
Western Juniper	55	--	--	--	55
Juniper woodland	254	25	29	1,318	1,626
Pinyon / juniper woodland	461	410	334	4,440	5,644
White fir	--	--	--	83	83
Subalpine fir	--	--	--	21	21
Limber pine	--	--	--	31	31
Aspen	--	--	31	--	31
Deciduous oak woodland	--	75	--	--	75
Cercocarpus woodland	29	37	21	178	265
All types	799	547	414	6,071	7,831

Data Table NV 2 -- Gross annual growth, annual mortality, and net annual growth of all trees on forest land by species, Nevada BLM land, 2005.

Species	Gross annual growth	Annual mortality	Net annual growth
	-------- Thousand cubic feet --------		
White fir	1,132	2,926	-1,794
Subalpine fir	200	--	200
Western juniper	45	--	45
Utah juniper	11,526	13,331	-1,805
Rocky Mountain juniper	14	--	14
Common or twoneedle pinyon	3	--	3
Limber pine	662	--	662
Singleleaf pinyon	20,054	26,544	-6,491
Great Basin bristlecone pine	24	--	24
Softwood total	33,659	42,802	-9,143
Curlleaf mountain-mahogany	1,070	1,438	-368
Aspen	137	--	137
Gambel oak	--	--	--
Hardwood total	1,207	1,438	-231
All species	34,866	44,240	-9,374

Data Table NM 1 -- Area of forest land by forest type and stand-size class, New Mexico BLM land, 2005.

Forest type	Stand-size class				
	Sparse stands (<10% stocked)	Seedlings/ saplings (0-4.9" dbh/ drc)	Medium trees (5-9" or 5-11" dbh/ drc)	Large trees (9 or 11"+ dbh/drc)	Total
	---------- Thousand acres ----------				
Juniper woodland	--	--	41	51	92
Pinyon / juniper woodland	19	24	306	598	946
Ponderosa pine	14	--	5	42	62
Deciduous oak woodland	--	9	--	6	15
Evergreen oak woodland	--	--	6	--	6
All types	33	33	358	696	1,121

Data Table NM 2 -- Gross annual growth, annual mortality, and net annual growth of all trees on forest land by species, New Mexico BLM land, 2005.

Species	Gross annual growth	Annual mortality	Net annual growth
	-------- Thousand cubic feet --------		
Alligator juniper	60	--	60
Utah juniper	516	--	516
Rocky Mountain juniper	228	--	228
Oneseed juniper	1,478	--	1,478
Common or twoneedle pinyon	2,864	79	2,786
Ponderosa pine	948	369	578
Border pinyon	--	--	--
Douglas-fir	41	2,265	-2,224
Softwood total	6,135	2,713	3,422
Arizona white oak/gray oak	3	--	3
Gambel oak	153	--	153
Oak, evergreen	5	--	5
Hardwood total	161	--	161
All species	6,296	2,713	3,583

Data Table OR 1 -- Area of forest land by forest type and stand-size class, Oregon and Washington BLM land, 2005.

Forest type	Sparse stands (<10% stocked)	Seedlings/ saplings (0-4.9" dbh/ drc)	Medium trees (5-9" or 5-11" dbh/drc)	Large trees (9 or 11"+ dbh/drc)	Total
	- - - - - - - - - Thousand acres - - - - - - - - -				
Western Juniper	441	186	13	758	1,398
Douglas-fir	--	58	238	1,247	1,542
Port-Orford-cedar	--	--	--	4	4
Ponderosa pine	20	3	--	204	226
Sugar pine	--	--	--	18	18
White fir	--	--	--	34	34
Red fir	--	--	--	12	12
Grand fir	--	--	--	36	36
Lodgepole pine	--	61	10	--	71
Western hemlock	--	--	2	34	36
Western redcedar	--	--	--	14	14
Western larch	--	--	13	--	13
Aspen	--	16	9	--	26
Red alder	--	3	9	16	29
Bigleaf maple	--	16	16	--	32
Oregon white oak	--	36	84	14	134
Canyon live oak / interior live oak	--	4	14	20	37
Tanoak	--	27	--	--	27
Giant chinkapin	--	19	29	--	48
Pacific madrone	--	16	29	41	86
Cercocarpus woodland	--	14	--	16	30
Nonstocked	14	--	--	--	14
All types	475	458	467	2,468	3,868

Data Table UT 1 -- Area of forest land by forest type and stand-size class, Utah BLM land, 2005.

Forest type	Sparse stands (<10% stocked)	Seedlings/saplings (0-4.9" dbh/drc)	Medium trees (5-9" or 5-11" dbh/drc)	Large trees (9 or 11"+ dbh/drc)	Total
	Stand-size class				
	---------- Thousand acres ----------				
Rocky Mountain juniper	--	--	--	51	51
Juniper woodland	300	51	41	1,506	1,898
Pinyon / juniper woodland	280	156	88	4,703	5,227
Douglas-fir	--	20	11	52	82
Ponderosa pine	10	--	--	41	51
Subalpine fir	--	--	--	8	8
Limber pine	10	--	--	--	10
Cottonwood	18	6	--	10	34
Aspen	--	9	--	2	11
Deciduous oak woodland	11	284	1	4	300
Cercocarpus woodland	10	9	30	96	146
Intermountain maple woodland	--	--	--	8	8
All types	639	535	171	6,481	7,825

Data Table UT 2 -- Gross annual growth, annual mortality, and net annual growth of all trees on forest land by species, Utah BLM land, 2005.

Species	Gross annual growth	Annual mortality	Net annual growth	
	- - - - - - Thousand cubic feet - - -			
White fir	210	1,416	-1,206	
Subalpine fir	248	644	-397	
Utah juniper	13,611	4,829	8,782	
Rocky Mountain juniper	465	5	459	
Engelmann spruce	10	--	10	
Common or twoneedle pinyon	9,621	7,853	1,767	
Limber pine	40	--	40	
Ponderosa pine	686	2,328	-1,642	
Singleleaf pinyon	3,777	2,780	997	
Great Basin bristlecone pine	6	--	6	
Douglas-fir	2,655	3,871	-1,216	
Softwood total	31,327	23,727	7,600	
Bigtooth maple	385	--	385	
Curlleaf mountain-mahogany	742	276	466	
Aspen	81	--	81	
Fremont cottonwood,Rio Grande cottonwood	104	--	104	
Narrowleaf cottonwood	135	--	135	
Gambel oak	428	17	411	
Hardwood total	1,875	292	1,582	
All species	33,202	24,019	9,182	

Data Table WY 1 -- Area of forest land by forest type and stand-size class, Wyoming BLM land, 2005.

Forest type	Sparse stands (<10% stocked)	Seedlings/ saplings (0-4.9" dbh/ drc)	Medium trees (5-9" or 5-11" dbh/drc)	Large trees (9 or 11"+ dbh/drc)	Total
	--------- Thousand acres ---------				
Juniper woodland	138	21	4	456	619
Pinyon / juniper woodland	6	--	--	11	17
Douglas-fir	--	--	14	51	65
Ponderosa pine	21	--	11	63	95
Engelmann spruce	--	--	4	--	4
Engelman spruce / subalpine fir	--	9	37	22	67
Lodgepole pine	8	11	39	28	85
Limber pine	69	61	43	40	212
Whitebark pine	--	3	--	9	11
Cottonwood	4	--	--	--	4
Sugarberry / hackberry / elm / green ash	--	--	6	--	6
Aspen	--	30	41	6	77
Cercocarpus woodland	10	6	--	9	25
All types	256	141	200	694	1,290

Data Table WY 2 -- Gross annual growth, annual mortality, and net annual growth of all trees on forest land by species, Wyoming BLM land, 2005.

Species	Gross annual growth	Annual mortality	Net annual growth
	--------- Thousand cubic feet -------		
Subalpine fir	4,103	1,839	2,264
Utah juniper	767	104	663
Rocky Mountain juniper	555	67	488
Engelmann spruce	284	--	284
Whitebark pine	323	--	323
Common or twoneedle pinyon	3	--	3
Lodgepole pine	4,012	786	3,226
Limber pine	1,844	725	1,119
Ponderosa pine	1,823	940	883
Douglas-fir	2,452	2,186	266
Softwood total	16,165	6,646	9,519
Boxelder	136	--	136
Rocky Mountain maple	--	--	--
Curlleaf mountain-mahogany	42	--	42
Aspen	2,095	913	1,181
Narrowleaf cottonwood	--	--	--
Hardwood total	2,273	913	1,359
All species	18,438	7,560	10,878

Appendix B
BLM Forest Lands in Alaska

Forest Type	BLM	Native-Selected *	State-Selected**	Total Acres
Black Spruce	7,603,607	3,223,095	3,843,301	14,670,003
White Spruce	6,980,390	4,928,657	5,243,323	17,152,369
Paper Birch	1,385,644	802,148	873,560	3,061,353
Aspen	232,367	392,132	100,956	725,455
Balsam Poplar	84,076	56,045	32,586	172,707
Mountain Hemlock	17,621	184,893	39,243	241,756
Cottonwood	10,672	44,416	9,915	65,003
Western Hemlock	6,903	162,267	39,243	208,413
Sitka Spruce	5,807	73,342	10,502	89,651
Alaska-yellow-cedar	494	14,888	2,749	18,131
Willow	170	154	0	324
Western Redcedar	15	32,617	4,201	36,833
Lodgepole Pine	0	4,170	124	4,293
Cottonwood/Willow	0	170	556	726
Grand Totals***	16,327,766	9,918,996	10,200,257	36,447,018

* **Native-Selected** lands are currently managed by the BLM, but a large proportion will be transferred to native corporations through the Alaska Native Claims Settlement Act (ANCSA). As of September 2006, approximately 6.3 million acres (forested and non-forested) have yet to be conveyed to native corporations. Lands that are selected, but not conveyed, will be administered permanently by the BLM.

** **State-Selected** lands are currently managed by the BLM, but a large proportion will be transferred to the State of Alaska through the Alaska Statehood Act. As of September 2006, approximately 10.9 million acres (forested and non-forested) have yet to be conveyed to the State of Alaska. Lands that are selected, but not conveyed, will be administered permanently by the BLM.

The target date for completion of both of these transfers is 2009.

*** Grand Totals will not equal portions due to rounding errors.

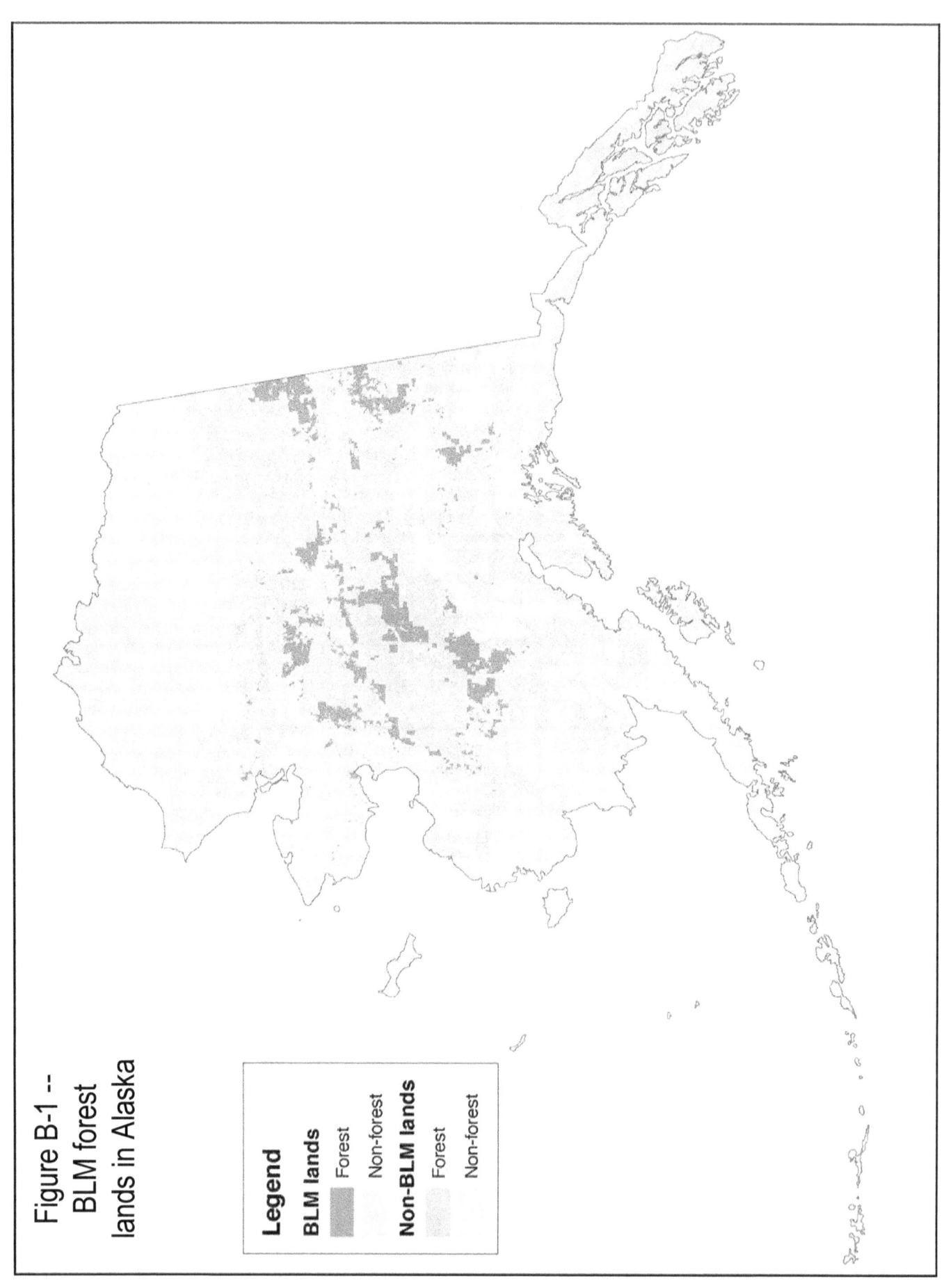

Figure B-1 --
BLM forest
lands in Alaska

Legend

BLM lands

Forest

Non-forest

Non-BLM lands

Forest

Non-forest

Appendix C
All Forest Types Acreage on BLM Land by State

Forest Type	Total	AZ	CA	CO	ID
Pinyon / juniper woodland	16,034,527	1,015,050	303,224	2,852,113	28,972
Juniper woodland	5,719,219	520,219	136,615	652,783	139,655
Western Juniper	1,947,558	0	277,895	0	216,921
Coastal Douglas-fir	1,496,756	0	16,927	0	0
Interior Douglas-fir	1,156,259	0	0	243,528	267,004
Ponderosa pine	1,072,133	12,772	0	158,769	0
Deciduous oak woodland	964,765	9,579	7,904	557,958	0
Cercocarpus woodland	642,001	0	67,279	20,272	51,757
Rocky Mountain juniper	433,288	0	0	184,881	41,560
Aspen	367,837	0	0	186,794	36,718
Lodgepole pine	359,306	0	0	93,819	0
Mesquite woodland	323,025	295,722	27,303	0	0
Limber pine	275,994	0	0	3,220	0
Canyon live oak / interior live oak	269,237	0	232,176	0	0
Oregon white oak	179,198	0	45,280	0	0
White fir	117,448	0	0	0	0
Engelman spruce / subalpine fir	106,655	0	0	0	0
Subalpine fir	99,751	0	0	41,247	28,852
Grand fir	98,831	0	0	0	62,999
Blue oak	90,474	0	90,474	0	0
Pacific madrone	86,288	0	0	0	0
Cottonwood	79,277	0	0	14,588	26,379
Tanoak	76,004	0	49,407	0	0
Engelmann spruce	74,830	0	0	66,468	0
California mixed conifer	74,258	0	74,258	0	0
Giant chinkapin	48,142	0	0	0	0
Nonstocked	45,033	0	31,263	0	0
Western hemlock	36,144	0	0	0	0
Bigleaf maple	32,493	0	0	0	0
Misc. western hardwood woodland	32,234	17,105	15,129	0	0
Paper birch	29,216	0	0	0	29,216
Red alder	28,643	0	0	0	0
Evergreen oak woodland	28,535	22,992	0	0	0
Whitebark pine	26,742	0	0	0	15,277
California black oak	24,114	0	24,114	0	0
Gray pine	20,510	0	20,510	0	0
Sugar pine	18,462	0	0	0	0
Misc. western softwoods	17,225	0	17,225	0	0
Western redcedar	13,821	0	0	0	0
Western larch	13,289	0	0	0	0
Red fir	12,185	0	0	0	0
Cottonwood / willow	10,784	0	10,784	0	0
Intermountain maple woodland	8,260	0	0	0	0
Sugarberry / hackberry / elm / green ash	7,524	0	0	0	0
Mixed upland hardwood	7,391	0	0	0	0
White spruce	7,283	0	0	0	0
Bur oak	6,450	0	0	0	0
Port-Orford-cedar	4,024	0	0	0	0
Oregon ash	1,430	0	1,430	0	0
Total	32,624,853	1,893,439	1,449,197	5,076,439	945,309

MT	NV	NM	ND	OR	SD	UT	WA	WY
0	5,644,277	946,274	0	0	0	5,227,447	0	17,171
35,411	1,625,783	91,968	0	0	0	1,897,674	0	619,112
0	55,074	0	0	1,397,669	0	0	0	0
0	0	0	0	1,479,830	0	0	0	0
435,984	0	0	0	13,804	0	81,980	48,690	65,268
454,194	0	61,952	0	226,386	11,661	50,994	0	95,406
0	74,848	14,802	0	0	0	299,673	0	0
37,476	264,972	0	0	29,908	0	145,509	0	24,827
153,822	0	0	1,924	0	0	51,100	0	0
0	30,658	0	0	25,664	0	10,919	0	77,085
109,565	0	0	0	70,712	0	0	0	85,210
0	0	0	0	0	0	0	0	0
20,235	30,941	0	0	0	0	9,501	0	212,096
0	0	0	0	37,061	0	0	0	0
0	0	0	0	117,071	0	0	16,847	0
0	83,274	0	0	34,174	0	0	0	0
39,227	0	0	0	0	0	0	0	67,428
0	21,391	0	0	0	0	8,260	0	0
0	0	0	0	35,832	0	0	0	0
0	0	0	0	0	0	0	0	0
0	0	0	0	86,288	0	0	0	0
0	0	0	0	0	0	33,973	0	4,338
0	0	0	0	26,597	0	0	0	0
4,076	0	0	0	0	0	0	0	4,287
0	0	0	0	0	0	0	0	0
0	0	0	0	48,142	0	0	0	0
0	0	0	0	13,770	0	0	0	0
0	0	0	0	36,144	0	0	0	0
0	0	0	0	32,493	0	0	0	0
0	0	0	0	0	0	0	0	0
0	0	0	0	0	0	0	0	0
0	0	0	0	28,643	0	0	0	0
0	0	5,543	0	0	0	0	0	0
0	0	0	0	0	0	0	0	11,465
0	0	0	0	0	0	0	0	0
0	0	0	0	0	0	0	0	0
0	0	0	0	18,462	0	0	0	0
0	0	0	0	0	0	0	0	0
0	0	0	0	13,821	0	0	0	0
0	0	0	0	0	0	0	13,289	0
0	0	0	0	12,185	0	0	0	0
0	0	0	0	0	0	0	0	0
0	0	0	0	0	0	8,260	0	0
0	0	0	1,054	0	0	0	0	6,470
0	0	0	7,391	0	0	0	0	0
0	0	0	0	0	7,283	0	0	0
0	0	0	0	0	6,450	0	0	0
0	0	0	0	4,024	0	0	0	0
0	0	0	0	0	0	0	0	0
1,289,991	7,831,219	1,120,539	10,369	3,788,679	25,394	7,825,290	78,826	1,290,162